RSA
COMPUTER LITERACY *and* INFORMATION TECHNOLOGY

 Heinemann Educational Books
in association with the RSA Examinations Board

Heinemann Educational,
a division of Heinemann Educational Books Ltd
Halley Court, Jordan Hill, Oxford OX2 8EJ

OXFORD LONDON EDINBURGH
MADRID ATHENS BOLOGNA PARIS
MELBOURNE SYDNEY AUCKLAND SINGAPORE TOKYO
IBADAN NAIROBI HARARE GABORONE
PORTSMOUTH NH (USA)

First published 1988
Reprinted 1988, 1989 (twice), 1990, 1991

British Library Cataloguing in Publication Data

RSA Computer literacy and information technology
  1. Business firms. Applications of computer systems
  I. Royal Society of Arts
  658'.05

ISBN 0-435-45183-9

Designed and produced by
The Pen and Ink Book Company Ltd,
Huntingdon, Cambridgeshire

Printed and bound in Spain by
Mateu Cromo

Also available:
**RSA Computer Literacy and
Information Technology Tutor's Resource Pack**

CONTENTS

ACKNOWLEDGEMENTS

The author and publishers would like to thank the following for permission to reproduce photographs on the pages indicated:

British Broadcasting Corporation: p.40.
British Telecom: p.40.
Oracle Teletext Ltd: p.40.

Thanks are also due to the following who gave permission to reproduce photographs on the front cover:

Spectrum colour library,
ZEFA

Special thanks to Fraser Bird who took the photographs for the 'In Action' pages in each unit.

The RSA's scheme in Computer Literacy and Information Technology (CLAIT) was introduced in the 1983–4 session. Its popularity has increased rapidly so that, in the last session alone, over 32,000 candidates were registered for the scheme. In recent years RSA has become a leader in the field of Information Technology qualifications for both students and teachers.

The CLAIT scheme was developed in response to demand for accreditation of basic, practical, computing and information technology skills. It had become evident that nearly everyone would soon need to be able to use computer terminals in business and industry and even in daily life. Most people did not want or need to know about the theoretical side of computing. The skills tested in the scheme are those practical ones needed to use, at a basic level, word processing, spreadsheet, database, videotex, graphics and business/accounting software on a computer system.

This book explains each of the computer applications which the scheme covers and gives realistic examples of their use in business and industry. It then provides tasks which have been designed to build up students' skills gradually and also give them practice in the type of assignments they will meet in their RSA assessment. A Tutor's Resource Pack has also been prepared to complement the Students' Book; this includes further tasks and support material for tutors.

The text has been prepared by Veronica Anderson and Gaynor Attwood, to whom the RSA here records its thanks. RSA also wishes to thank the firms which allowed their experiences with information technology to be used in the book.

Martin Cross
Chief Executive
RSA Examinations Board

INTRODUCTION

This book is to help you understand how computers are used to process information in business and industry. The skills you will practise are those needed in many jobs; they are also becoming necessary in everyday life, for example home shopping and personal finance.

It has been written primarily for students preparing for RSA's Computer Literacy and Information Technology (CLAIT) scheme, but it can be used by anyone who wants a practical introduction to computers in information technology. You may be using this book with, or without, the help of a teacher or tutor. If you are working alone you will need to refer to your computer manual to find out the exact instructions for your machine. This book cannot give you these instructions because of the very many different types of equipment and programs which are used.

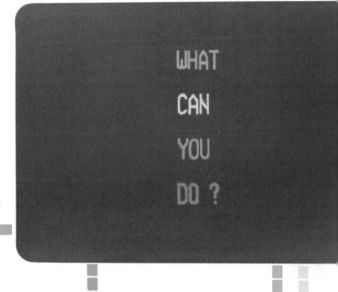

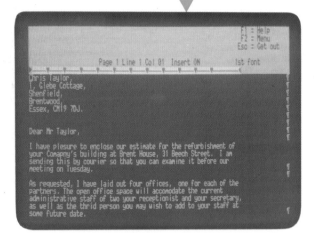

You can use *word processing* to key in documents and save and store them. The work can then be printed or changes can be made at a later stage.

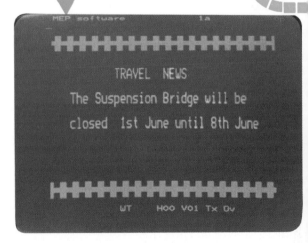

You can use a *videotex* system to display information which can be looked at by other people.

CLAIT covers the six most common applications of computers: word processing, spreadsheets, databases, videotex, business/accounting and graphics/plotting. The pictures below show examples of how each can be used.

Using a *spreadsheet* package, you can enter data, perform calculations and 'experiment' with changing the values.

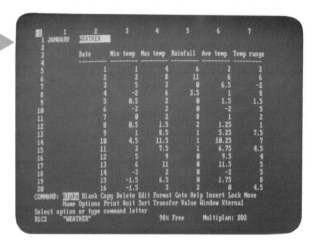

There are many different *business* and *accounting* packages which you can use to keep financial records, record stock changes, etc.

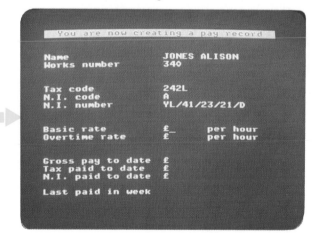

Databases are used to store records so that information can be extracted quickly and easily.

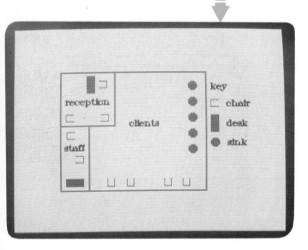

Graphics and *plotting* packages allow you to draw plans and pictures and display figures in graphical form.

HOW TO USE THIS BOOK

This book is divided into seven main units. You will find them on the pages given below:

UNITS 1–6

Each of the first six units is completely independent. You can use them in any order. In each one there is:

- **a general explanation** of the computer package.

- **an example** of how the computer package can be used in business or industry.

- **exercises** to help you build up your skills, and **complete assignments** so that you can practise for the RSA assessment and check your own performance. (The mix of exercises and assignments depends on the needs in each unit.)

- a **Command Checklist** for you to complete. (This forms a reference sheet which tells you how to carry out the basic functions on **your** package.)

UNIT 7

The seventh unit is **very important**. You will need to look at it as soon as you start to use the computer and also when you look at each of the Units 1–6. It concerns the use of the computer systems themselves, rather than the use of any individual package.

In Units 1–6 words may be used which you do not understand. Many of these will be explained in Unit 7. If there are words which you still do not understand, then you should:

- ask your **tutor**.
- look in your **manual**.
- look them up in an **Information Technology dictionary** or glossary.

TASKS

All the tasks in the book have numbers printed down the right-hand and left-hand sides. These relate to the **RSA Computer Literacy and Information Technology (CLAIT) Scheme** (see page 89), for which this book has been written. If you are not planning to take the RSA assessment you can ignore the numbers down the sides of the tasks and need not study 'Some Questions and Answers on the RSA CLAIT Scheme' on page 5.

TUTOR'S RESOURCE PACK

There is a **Tutor's Resource Pack** (also published by Heinemann Educational Books in association with RSA Examinations Board) which goes with this Students' Book. Your tutor may have that resource pack and will be able to give you more exercises, assignments and support material. If not, don't worry as this book is complete in itself.

Enjoy using the computer and good luck with your assessment!

SOME QUESTIONS AND ANSWERS ON THE RSA CLAIT SCHEME

? How much of the scheme must I cover?

A Of the six applications available (word processing, spreadsheet, database, videotex, business/accounting, graphics/plotting) you can choose to attempt any number–from just one to all six.

? How is my performance assessed?

A You have to show your Local Assessor (probably your own tutor) and the RSA exactly what skills you have acquired. To do this you must carry out an assignment for each of the applications you have chosen. This will be a practical task, carried out on the computer. You will not have to answer theoretical questions or write essays for this scheme.

? How do I know what standard the RSA requires?

A Look at the syllabus on pages 89–92 of this book. The **assessment objectives** list exactly what you must do. The **criteria of assessment** on page 92 explain that:
- when keying in material you must make no more than three errors in any one assignment;
- you must carry out all the other operations listed with complete accuracy.

? What certificate will I get?

A You will receive a certificate which lists **profile sentences** detailing exactly what you have achieved on the CLAIT scheme. If you meet all the basic requirements for three applications your certificate will state that you have passed at **Stage I**. If, in addition, you successfully carry out a few specific extra requirements for each application, you will pass at **Stage I with Distinction**.

? What is a Profile Sentence?

A Look at the syllabus again and find the Profile Sentences listed on each page. It is these sentences (or at least some of them) which will appear on your certificate. To be awarded a Profile Sentence you must prove that you can achieve each of the corresponding objectives. For example, the Profile Sentence P1, below, describes the three operations listed as Assessment Objectives 01, 02 and 03:

Topics	Assessment Objectives	Profile Sentences
	Candidates must be able to demonstrate ability to	
(a) A Word Processing package	01 **ENTER** text 02 **LOAD** text 03 **SAVE** text	P1 Enter, load and save text.

If you demonstrate successfully, in the course of your assignment, that you can enter, load and save text, then your certificate will list this Profile Sentence. Thus you will have an official record of what you can actually do. For example:

```
SUSAN G PENDRILL has demonstrated the ability to:

APPLICATIONS OF COMPUTERS AND INFORMATION TECHNOLOGY
-------------------------------------------------------------

WORD PROCESSING
Enter, load and save text.
```

1 WORD PROCESSING OVERVIEW

WHAT IS WORD PROCESSING?

Word processing allows you to enter text into a computer system. Both the text and its appearance can be altered. We refer to changes in the text as editing or amending, and changes in its appearance (e.g. line spacing) as formatting. The text can be stored on disc and printed out when required.

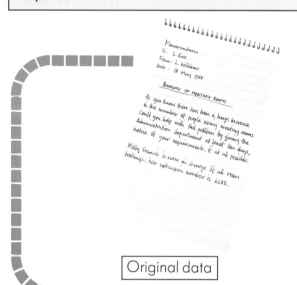

Original data

CPU

Input via keyboard

EDITING

This term covers the variety of operations which you use to make changes and corrections to text which has been entered or recalled.

PARTS OF A WORD PROCESSING SYSTEM

MONITOR or VDU (Visual Display Unit)	DISCS	DISC DRIVE

This is the screen on which the text can be seen as it is keyed in to the word processor. The line length on the screen display usually allows for 40 or 80 letters, figures and spaces. As well as showing the text as it is entered, a *cursor* indicates where the next character keyed in will appear. The cursor may appear as a box or a line, and may or may not be flashing. The name of the document, and other information may also be given on the screen.

The text files are stored on a disc. The word processing program may also be stored on a disc. The size of the disc will depend on the type of word processor system used.

The disc is inserted into the disc drive so that text can be written to, or read from, the disc. The disc drive enables documents and files to be saved on the disc and allows any text already stored on disc to be loaded into the word processing system when required.

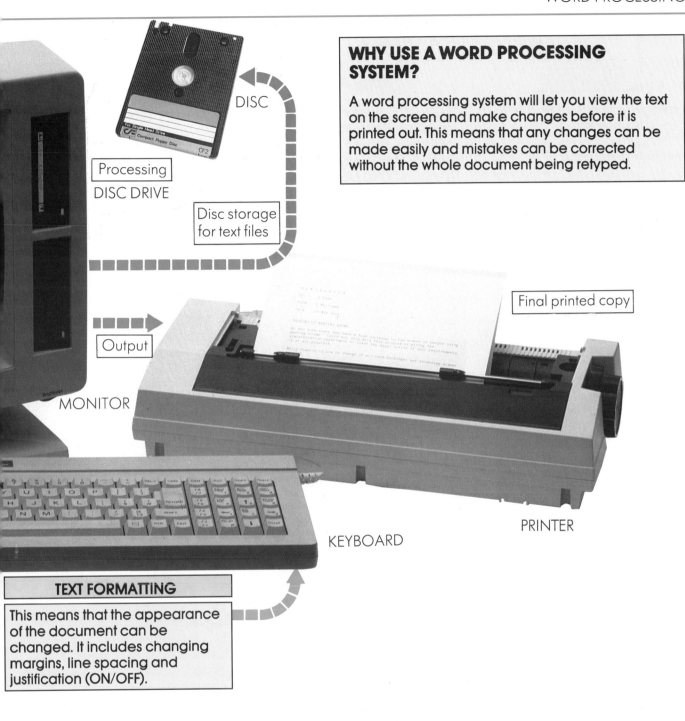

DISC

Processing
DISC DRIVE

Disc storage
for text files

WHY USE A WORD PROCESSING SYSTEM?

A word processing system will let you view the text on the screen and make changes before it is printed out. This means that any changes can be made easily and mistakes can be corrected without the whole document being retyped.

Output

Final printed copy

MONITOR

PRINTER

KEYBOARD

TEXT FORMATTING

This means that the appearance of the document can be changed. It includes changing margins, line spacing and justification (ON/OFF).

KEYBOARD	PRINTER	CPU (Central Processing Unit)
This is the main input device of a word processor, for entering data. The alphabetic keys are usually set out in the QWERTY layout. There may be an additional numeric keypad and normally there are extra keys to allow the operator to call up additional word processing facilities.	A copy of the text held in the word processing system can be printed out by the printer. There are many different types of printer; the most common are dot matrix and daisy wheel.	This is the 'heart' of the computer or word processing system. It is the link between the input and output devices and the memory and enables them to work efficiently.

PROCESSING THE TEXT

TEXT EDITING

Editing facilities enable the word processing operator to insert or delete single characters, words, sentences and paragraphs. Some systems offer an overwrite facility so that, as new work is inserted, it replaces whatever was there before.

TEXT FORMATTING

Formatting features include:

- changing the line spacing.
- changing the left-hand and right-hand margins.
- presenting the text with justification on or off.

What is justification?
If justification is **on** then the text will be presented straight at both margins, right and left-hand. Text which is not right-justified (i.e. justification is **off**) will appear with the right-hand edge 'ragged'.

Not all text formatting instructions appear on the VDU, but they will be taken into account when the document is printed. The screens and printout show the effect of some of these editing and formatting procedures on a short piece of text.

THE SCREENS

The text on screen 1 has several mistakes. These have been edited on screen 2 and also the text has been reformatted. The line length has been increased by changing both margins and the text has been right-justified.

Screen 1

Screen 2

THE PRINTOUT

The printout shows the text from screen 2. An instruction had been given to print in double line spacing but this was not displayed on the screen. The result can, however, be seen on the printout.

The usefulness of individual computers can be increased dramatically by enabling them to communicate with each other. The communication can be by way of a network or a modem.

WORD PROCESSING TERMS

WORD WRAP

A word that is too long to fit on the end of a line is carried over to the next line.

AUTOMATIC REFORMATTING

Changes in the way the text is formatted can be seen on the screen as soon as a formatting instruction is given.

WYSIWYG

An acronym for What You See Is What You Get. A system is WYSIWYG if the display on the screen looks the same as the printout. Not all word processing systems are WYSIWYG.

EMBEDDED COMMANDS

'Codes' that are inserted into the text to determine the format of the printed text. They can be seen on the screen as symbols but do not appear in the printout.

SCROLLING

The movement of text up, down or across the screen. Scrolling is necessary when the text is too large for it all to be shown on the screen at once.

SEARCH AND REPLACE

A feature which allows one word or phrase to be exchanged for another. The instruction can apply to just one occurrence of the word, to a specified number of occurrences or throughout a document.

MAILSHOT/MAILMERGE

The combining, at print, of data from two files. This usually involves inserting names and addresses from one file into a standard letter in another file.

WORD PROCESSING IN ACTION

Mason & Moore Dutton is a firm of solicitors in Chester. It has five Partners, and a number of other staff including secretarial and clerical personnel. The work is varied and includes conveyancing and preparation of wills and leases.

In 1986 the firm installed an Olivetti ETV word processing system. It is a screen-based system with floppy-disc drives and a daisy-wheel printer. Liz Guest has been using the system since it was installed. It took her a little while to get used to the differences from a typewriter, but now she talks enthusiastically about the advantages that word processing has brought to her work.

Many of the documents I produce are wills and leases; they are all very similar. When they were prepared on the typewriter each one had to be typed individually. Now I can simply save the standard clauses on disc, call up the appropriate ones, compile them into a document and insert the variable information, such as names and addresses of the particular client.

The same applies to the documents from the Conveyancing Department. Many of these are very complicated and have to go through several versions before the clients agree a final version. That meant the *whole* document was re-typed a number of times. Now the document can be stored, recalled and amended – so only the actual changes have to be re-typed. It saves so much time and frustration! Also, the documents I produce look really professional as the printer is of a very high quality.

Diana Williams, one of the Partners, repeated Liz's comments about saving time:

This really is a cost-effective use of human resources; more secretarial time is spent on "new" work instead of re-typing. We are now using word processing for affidavits, building society possession orders and correspondence – some of which relates to our debt collecting service. I can't imagine how we would manage without such a system now!

BUILD-UP EXERCISES

TASK 1

WHAT'S THIS TASK FOR?

This task is designed to allow you to practise the skills required to gain CLAIT Profile Sentence

P1	Enter, load and save text.

BEFORE YOU BEGIN

You will need to find out and note down how to:

- ○ load your word processing program.
- ○ enter text.
- ○ save text.
- ○ use a keyboard.
- ○ load paper into the printer, set paper and printer to the top of a form.
- ○ check the printer is on-line.
- ○ output hard copy.

> The numbers (e.g. 01) that you see on the left-hand side of the page show the CLAIT word-processing objectives. The numbers that you see on the right-hand side show the CLAIT objectives relating to the use of the system.

	1 Load your word-processing program.	057
01	**2** Key in the text below with an UNJUSTIFIED right-hand margin:	060

REDECORATING A HOUSE

Home decoration opens up great possibilities for the practical, for not only is the work easy, but there is something concrete to show for the labour.

If the worker is a novice he should start work on a relatively unimportant room to gain experience before venturing on any of the main rooms in the house.

The importance of obtaining the very best materials cannot be over-emphasised, as good work cannot be expected from cheap and usually inferior materials, be they paint, wallpaper or anything else.

03	**3** Save your file and print a copy.	062, 063

TASK 2

WHAT'S THIS TASK FOR?

In this task you will practise for CLAIT Profile Sentence

P2	Insert/delete/replace words; insert/delete paragraphs.

BEFORE YOU BEGIN

You will need to find out and note down how to:

- ○ load text.
- ○ insert words.
- ○ insert a paragraph.
- ○ delete words.
- ○ delete a paragraph.
- ○ replace words.

02	**1**	Reload the text from Task 1. In the first paragraph:
04		**a** insert the word **person** after **practical** and before the comma
04		**b** insert the words **profitable and interesting**, following the word **easy,**
07	**2**	Delete the paragraph beginning **If the worker ...**
05	**3**	Insert the following paragraph after the first paragraph:

Today there are many books and leaflets which will be
useful if you have never attempted this type of work
before. However, it is a good idea to refresh your
memory by browsing through such guidance, even if you
have carried out such work previously.

	4	In the paragraph beginning **The importance of ...:**
04		**a** insert **and lasting** following the word **good**
06		**b** delete **cheap and usually** following the words **expected from**
06		**c** delete from **be they paint ...** to the paragraph end
08		**d** replace the comma following **materials** with a full stop
03	**5**	Save your file and print one copy.

062, 063

TASK 3

WHAT'S THIS TASK FOR?

This task is designed to allow you to practise the
skills required to gain CLAIT Profile Sentences

P1	Enter, load and save text.
P3	Change margins.
P4	Change layout.

BEFORE YOU BEGIN

You will need to find out and note down how to:

- change the left margin.
- change the right margin.
- change the line-spacing.
- use an unjustified right-hand margin.
- use justified margins.

01	**1**	Key in the text below with an UNJUSTIFIED right-hand margin:

060

FINISHING A PLANED SURFACE

To produce a greater degree of smoothness than can
be obtained by a sharp plane, smooth the work with
glasspaper. This material, as its name implies,
consists of strong paper upon which finely
powdered glass is glued. It can be bought in
various degrees of coarseness and it is best used
wrapped round a wooden block. Glasspaper must be
worked in the direction of the grain of the wood.

03	**2**	Save your file and print a copy.
02	**3**	Recall the text and reformat it as follows:
★010		**a** double-line spacing
★011		**b** justified right-hand margin
09		**c** move BOTH margins in by 10 characters
03	**4**	Save your file and print a copy.

062, 063

062, 063

COMMAND CHECKLIST

Complete the list below, referring to any notes you made while carrying out Tasks 1, 2 and 3. You can then use your list as a reference sheet to complete the tasks that follow.

OBJECTIVE	HOW DO I DO IT?
01 Enter text	
02 Load text	
03 Save text	
04 Insert words	
05 Insert paragraph	
06 Delete words	
07 Delete paragraph	
08 Replace words	
09 Change margins	
★010 Vary line spacing	
★011 Justification: on	
off	

You may also wish to make a note of the default settings of your word processing program.

	DEFAULT SETTING
Left margin	
Right margin	
Line length	
Page length	
Line spacing	
Justification (on or off)	

RSA ASSIGNMENTS & SELF-ASSESSMENTS

TASK 4

WHAT'S THIS TASK FOR?

This task allows you to practise a complete CLAIT assignment. All the CLAIT word processing objectives are covered and some of the CLAIT objectives relating to the use of the system are included.

	1	Power up the system and load your word processing program.	056, 057
01	**2**	Open a file and enter the following text using an unjustified right-hand margin.	060

THE FOOD YOU EAT

There is an increasing interest in all aspects of the foods we eat and the effect that they have on our bodies. One important element has been identified that poses a danger in our daily life - fast food, lacking vitamins and protein.

Good eating habits help to maintain good health. Poor eating habits - for example, canteen meals and quick snacks - may lead to health problems such as overweight and high blood pressure - well-known risk factors.

You can take steps to prevent damage to your health, you may wish to follow the clear and simple advice outlined below.

Avoid eating too much fat such as butter, oil, cake, chocolate, potato crisps, eggs, nuts and cheese. Avoid fried foods.

Eat foods high in fibre such as wholemeal breads and cereals, fresh vegetables and fruits, peas, beans, pulses and seeds.

Drink plenty of water instead of cordials and soft drinks; drink alcohol in moderation.

03	**3**	Save your file.	
	4	Load the printer with paper and set to top of form, check the printer is on-line and print the document.	061, 062, 063
02, 09	**5**	Reload your file, and set in your right- and left-hand margins by 5 characters.	
07	**6**	Delete the first paragraph beginning **There is an increasing ...**	
	7	In the paragraph beginning **Good eating habits ...**	
06	**a**	delete the words **canteen meals and**	
04	**b**	insert a comma after the word **overweight** and then insert the words **high blood fats (cholesterol)** before the words **and high blood pressure**	
08	**8**	In the paragraph beginning **You can take steps ...** replace the words **You can take steps to prevent damage to** with the words **In order to safeguard**	
05	**9**	Insert the following paragraph after the paragraph beginning **Eat foods high in fibre ...**	

Limit your intake of high salt foods such as cured, corned and canned meats, cheese, salami, and meat pastes. Be careful about the amount of the following that you consume - smoked and canned fish, vegetable extracts, many takeaway meals and snack foods.

03	**10**	Save your amended file and print one copy.	062, 063
02, ★010, ★011	**11**	Reload your file and reformat the text in double line spacing, with a justified right-hand margin.	
03	**12**	Save your file and print one copy.	062, 063
	13	Close down the system.	059

SELF-ASSESSMENT: TASK 4

DID I DO IT CORRECTLY?

- Entered text with no more than 3 data entry errors
- Loaded the text
- Saved the text
- Inserted a comma after the word **overweight** and inserted the words **high blood fats (cholesterol)**
- Inserted the paragraph beginning Limit your **intake of ...**
- Deleted the words **canteen meals and**

- Deleted the paragraph beginning **There is an increasing ...**
- Replaced the words **You can take steps to prevent damage to** with the words in **order to safeguard**
- Changed the right-hand margin
- Changed the left-hand margin
- Changed to double line spacing
- Justified the right-hand margin

If you did this task in two hours or less and have met each of the requirements listed above, you should be ready to take the CLAIT word processing assessment.

TASK 5

WHAT'S THIS TASK FOR?

This task, while covering all the CLAIT word processing objectives, is presented in a different format; i.e. the amendments are shown on copy, not given by instruction.

01	**1** Load your word processing program.	057
	2 Open a file and enter the text below:	060

GENERAL ADVICE ON REDECORATION

All portable furniture, ornaments, pictures, etc., should be removed from the room before starting work. Everything that cannot be conveniently removed should be covered with sheets of newspaper or dust sheets. This will protect any remaining furniture from stray splashes of paint from the ceiling.

Firstly, wipe down the old paintwork, repair any defects and paint the ceiling and frieze.

Secondly, apply a first (or under) coat of paint to the woodwork.

The next step is to repair any cracks in the plaster before hanging the new wallpaper.

Care must be taken in not only the selection of the wallpaper, but also in the way it is hung. Be careful, for instance, that you do not end up with one of the pieces placed upside down!

Lastly, apply the final coat of paint to the woodwork.

	3 Save your file.	
03	**4** Load paper into the printer, set to top of form and print a copy of the file with an unjustified right-hand margin.	061, 062, 063

02	**5**	Recall your file and amend it as shown:

REDECORATING A ROOM — A PLAN OF ACTION

08 ~~GENERAL ADVICE ON REDECORATION~~

```
All portable furniture, ornaments, pictures, etc., should be
removed  from the room before starting work. Everything that
cannot be conveniently removed should be covered with ~~sheets~~
```
06 ```
~~of newspaper or~~ dust sheets. This will protect any remaining
furniture from stray splashes of paint from the ceiling.
```

→ ```
Firstly, wipe down the old paintwork, repair any defects and
paint the ceiling and frieze.
```

```
Secondly,  apply  a  first (or under) coat of paint to  the
woodwork.
```
                              strip the old wallpaper and
04 ```
The next step is to repair any cracks in the plaster before
hanging the new wallpaper.
```

07 ~~Care must be taken in not only the selection of the wallpaper, but also in the way it is hung. Be careful, for instance, that you do not end up with one of the pieces placed upside down!~~

```
Lastly, apply the final coat of paint to the woodwork.
```

05 *If you are going to redecorate a room completely it is essential that you work in a planned and logical order so that you will not spoil any of the work you have already completed.*

09	**6**	Move the margins in by 5 characters on each side.	062, 063
03	**7**	Save the file.	059
★010, ★011	**8**	Print the document with a justified right-hand margin in double line spacing.	
	9	Close down the system.	

SELF-ASSESSMENT: TASK 5

DID I DO IT CORRECTLY?

- Entered text with no more than 3 data entry errors
- Loaded the text
- Saved the text
- Inserted the words **strip the old wallpaper and**
- Inserted the paragraph beginning **If you are going to ...**
- Deleted the words **sheets of newspaper or**
- Deleted the paragraph beginning **Care must be taken ...**

- Replaced the words **GENERAL ADVICE ON REDECORATION** with the words **REDECORATING A ROOM – A PLAN OF ACTION**
- Changed the right-hand margin
- Changed the left-hand margin
- Changed to double line spacing
- Justified the right-hand margin

If you did this task in two hours or less and have met each of the requirements listed above you should be ready to take the CLAIT word processing assessment.
```

WHAT IS A SPREADSHEET?

A spreadsheet allows you to enter and store data in a 'grid' format on a computer system. There are three main types of entry: numeric data, text and formulae.

- **Numeric data** – these are the numbers which will form the basis of the calculations that the program carries out for you.
- **Text** – this is made up of the words and headings on the spreadsheet.
- **Formulae** – these are the instructions which make the computer perform numeric calculations within the spreadsheet, e.g. add one entry to another entry.

COLUMN   LABEL

ROW

CELL

STATUS AREA

ROW	COLUMN	CELL
This is a line of cells **across** the spreadsheet. Each row has a reference number or letter.	This is a line of cells **down** the spreadsheet. In the diagram above the column references are letters of the alphabet. However, some spreadsheets use numbers for both rows **and** columns.	A single 'box' on the spreadsheet grid is called a **cell**. Each cell can be identified by giving its row and column reference. The reference C4 would mean that the cell is in column C and row 4; it is the cell where row 4 crosses column C.

WHY USE A SPREADSHEET?

With a spreadsheet you can perform calculations on the numbers that you have entered. The program carries out calculations according to the formulae which you have also entered. The spreadsheet will allow you to make amendments and changes quickly and easily. Any of the entries can be changed, including numeric data and formulae. The effects these changes have on the results of the calculations will be displayed automatically. You will not have to recalculate the figures yourself.

SCROLLING

A complete spreadsheet may well be too large for all of it to be shown at one time on the screen. You can scroll to the left and right or up and down until the part of the spreadsheet you want to see is visible.

The diagram opposite shows the screen boundary in blue; outside this boundary you can also see the full extent of the spreadsheet. If you wished to see column I on the screen you would need to scroll to the right.

— COMMAND LINE

	A	B	C	D	E	F	G	H	I	J
1:		JUL/84	OCT/84	JAN/85	APR/85	JUL/85	OCT/85	JAN/86	APR/86	JUL/86
2:	INCOME									
3	GOODS OUT	968.56	634 58	910 68	922 39	739 66	964 58	950.43	1298 00	1327.41
4:	INTEREST	350.00	350 00	350.00	350 00	350.00	350 00	350.00	350 00	350 00
5:	QUARTERLY TOTAL	1318.56	984.58	1260 68	1272.39	1089 66	1314 58	1300 43	1648 00	1677 41
6:	EXPENDITURE									
7:	OVERHEADS	650.00	650.00	650.00	650 00	650 00	650.00	650 00	650 00	650 00
8	WAGES	545.00	545.00	545.00	545.00	565.00	565 00	565 00	565 00	565.00
9:	GOODS IN	956.60	1067.50	1255.69	940.88	1046.44	1234.82	1395 37	1276 89	1361.71
10:	QUARTERLY TOTAL	2151 60	2262.50	2450.69	2135 88	2261 44	2449 82	2610 37	2491 89	2576 71
11										
12										
13:										
14:										
15:										
16:										
17:										

LABELS

The text entries on the spreadsheet are called labels. Text is normally kept to a minimum in the spreadsheet. It is mainly used to give names (headings) to the columns and rows so that, when the spreadsheet is studied, it is easier to make sense of the numeric data.

STATUS AREA

This area on the screen display gives information about the particular spreadsheet you are working on. The information it contains will vary from program to program. However, the status line is likely to include the contents of the cell being used, the name of the spreadsheet and the storage space remaining in the computer.

COMMAND LINE

This area on the screen display is usually just below the spreadsheet area. It displays the data or any commands as you key them in and before the ENTER or RETURN key is pressed.

GETTING THE DATA RIGHT

EDITING

The editing facility allows you to change figures, text or a formula on the spreadsheet. You may need to correct a mistake made when entering the data, or perhaps the circumstances have changed and the data needs revising.

REPLICATING

The replicating facility lets you copy an entry or a range of entries from one part of a spreadsheet to another. This can be very useful if, for instance, the same figure has to be entered at the same point in every column. You simply enter the figure once and then replicate it across the whole row.

SPREADSHEET LAYOUT

TEXT

The text displayed on a spreadsheet can be right-justified, left-justified or centred. Each cell, column and row can be set independently.

NUMERIC DATA

There are several ways in which numeric data can be displayed. With your spreadsheet program you may be able to choose:

- how many decimal places to display.
- to display in pound and pence format, i.e. with two decimal places.
- to display the data in **integer format**, i.e. rounding it to the nearest whole number.
- to justify your display to the right or to the left, although it is more common to justify numbers to the right.

USING FORMULAE

Formulae will allow you to multiply, divide, add and subtract the figures on your spreadsheet. When keying in the formulae you can use the + sign for addition and the − sign for subtraction, but multiplication is usually represented by the ★ sign and division by the / sign. The program will also recognise cell references and signs such as > (greater than) and < (less than). Your manual will give you exact instructions.

PRINTING OUT YOUR SPREADSHEET

When printing you are normally offered two options:

a   to print the spreadsheet as it appears on the screen, i.e. showing the figures you have entered and the results of any calculations carried out.

b   to print the 'contents' of the spreadsheet. This will show the various entries in each cell; these may be formulae, instead of the results of calculations as in (a) above.

You may be able to choose whether to print the whole spreadsheet or only part of it. You would need to give the column and row references of the part of the spreadsheet you want to print.

```
                  JUL/84   OCT/84   JAN/85   APR/8
INCOME
GOODS OUT           969      635      911
INTEREST            350      350      350
QUARTERLY TOTAL    1319      985     1261
EXPENDITURE
OVERHEADS           650      650
WAGES               545      545
GOODS IN            957     1068
QUARTERLY TOTAL    2152     2263
```

This is a printout of the spreadsheet in integer (i.e. whole number) format. The titles in the first column are left-justified; the entries in the remaining columns are right-justified.

PROJECTING A NEW VALUE

A major advantage of using a spreadsheet is that it quickly re-calculates the effects of changes to any of the entries on the spreadsheet. This is often referred to as the 'what if' facility. For example, WHAT would happen to the price of these goods IF the cost of the raw materials increased by 50 per cent? Projecting a new value allows you to find out the answers to such questions quickly.

This is a printout of the 'contents' of the spreadsheet. Only some of the contents have been selected—in this case the formulae used to calculate the quarterly totals for expenditure.

It is important to note that this is just one of several different methods of entering formulae on spreadsheets; you will need to find out exactly how your package operates.

```
SuperCalc ver.   1.00

B10         = SUM(B7:B9)
C10         = SUM(C7:C9)
D10         = SUM(D7:D9)
E10         = SUM(E7:E9)
F10         = SUM(F7:F9)
G10         = SUM(G7:G9)
```

SPREADSHEETS IN ACTION

The Royal Insurance head office is based in Liverpool. It is at this branch that Ray Watson runs the Financial Planning Division.

In the department everyone has access to an IBM personal computer. They use Lotus 123 for their work.

Because of the need for careful backup, the department uses a 20 MB tape streamer for backing up the data. This has equivalent storage capacity to 60 floppy discs. They also have an Epson FX105 plotter for the production of colour graphs, an Epson LQ2500, and a Kyocera laser printer.

Ray Watson explained:

The department has two main functions. The first is to collect and process the information from 34 branches all over the country. Each branch sends in its figures every month. These details are then entered into the spreadsheet program.

The details are used to prepare management reports so that it is possible to keep a close monitor on progress.

The second function is to carry out budgetary control. Here we compare the "actual" figures with the "target" figures. We can then make adjustments to those targets so that the branches can meet these requirements.

The main advantage of using a spreadsheet is the ability to carry out "experimental" work. This is work that previously would have taken many, many hours, if indeed it was possible at all. An example of this might be the ability to search quickly through the data to find which branches or departments have met their targets; it may be that there is an incentive bonus and this is even more effective if there is a quick turn-around on the results.

I have been using spreadsheets for a number of years, but I particularly like the Lotus program because it is easy to use and very powerful.

BUILD-UP EXERCISES

TASK 1

WHAT'S THIS TASK FOR?

This task is designed to allow you to practise the skills required to gain CLAIT Profile Sentence

P5	Enter and edit text and numeric data.

BEFORE YOU BEGIN

You will need to find out and note down how to:

- load your spreadsheet program.
- enter text.
- enter numeric data.
- delete entries.
- replace entries.

The numbers (e.g. 012) that you see on the left-hand side of the page show the CLAIT spreadsheet objectives. The numbers that you see on the right-hand side show the CLAIT objectives relating to the use of the system.

	#		
	1	Load your spreadsheet program.	057
012	2	Enter the heading **MEDAL TABLE**	060
012	3	Starting in the second column, enter the following headings:	060
		BRONZE SILVER GOLD TOTAL AVERAGE	
012	4	In the first column enter the following titles (left-justified):	060

NORTH
SOUTH
EAST
WEST
SCOTLAND
TOTAL

013	5	Enter the data shown below:	060

	BRONZE	SILVER	GOLD
NORTH	**12**	**23**	**19**
SOUTH	**15**	**4**	**3**
EAST	**7**	**14**	**18**
WEST	**14**	**3**	**10**
SCOTLAND	**10**	**6**	**11**

	6	Save your spreadsheet and print it.	062, 063
	7	There are errors in the data; make the following changes:	
015		**a** the **NORTH** gained **14 SILVER** medals	
015		**b** the **EAST** gained **19 BRONZE** medals	
014	8	The results for SCOTLAND are not to be included in the calculations, delete the **SCOTLAND** row.	
	9	Save and print the spreadsheet.	062, 063

TASK 2

WHAT'S THIS TASK FOR?

This task is designed to allow you to practise the skills required to gain CLAIT Profile Sentence

P8	Use formulae.

BEFORE YOU BEGIN

You will need to find out and note down how to:

- ○ use a formula.

	1	Load your spreadsheet data file from Task 1.	058
018	2	Use a formula to calculate:	
	a	the total number of medals for each area	
	b	the average number of medals for each area	
	c	the total number of each type of medal awarded	
	3	Save the spreadsheet and print two copies, one showing the figures and one showing the formulae.	062, 063

TASK 3

WHAT'S THIS TASK FOR?

This task is designed to allow you to practise the skills required to gain CLAIT Profile Sentences

P6	Replicate in a spreadsheet.
P7	Change the format.

BEFORE YOU BEGIN

You will need to find out and note down how to:

- ○ replicate entries.
- ○ change cell format.

	1	Load your spreadsheet program.	057
012	2	Enter the heading **POCKET MONEY**	060
012	3	Starting in the third column, enter the following headings:	060
		JAN FEB MAR APR MAY TOTAL	
012	4	In the first column enter the following titles (left-justified):	060
		PARENTS	
		WORK	
		GRANDPARENTS	
		OTHER	
		TOTAL	
013	5	Enter the data shown below using the replicate command:	060

	JAN	FEB	MAR	APR	MAY
PARENTS	15	15	15	15	15
WORK	12	12	12	12	12
GRANDPARENTS	5	5	5	5	5
OTHER		2		4	1

	6	Print your spreadsheet.	062, 063
017	7	Change the format to display to 2 decimal places.	

018	**8**	Use a formula to calculate:	
		a the **TOTAL** for **JAN.** Use the replicate command to calculate the **TOTAL** for months **FEB** to **MAY**.	
		b the **TOTAL** from **PARENTS**. Replicate the formula to calculate the **TOTAL** for **WORK**, **GRANDPARENTS** and **OTHER**.	
	9	Save your spreadsheet and print it.	062, 063

TASK 4

WHAT'S THIS TASK FOR?

This task is designed to allow you to practise the skills required to gain CLAIT Profile Sentence

| P9 | Extend the spreadsheet. |

BEFORE YOU BEGIN

You will need to find out and note down how to:

- add a row/column.
- project new values.

	1	Load your spreadsheet program.	057
012	**2**	Enter the heading **SALES FIGURES**	060
012	**3**	Starting in the third column, enter the following headings:	060

JAN	FEB	MAR	TOTAL NO	UNIT COST	AMOUNT

| 012 | **4** | In the first column enter the following titles (left-justified): | 060 |

KENT
WOODS
PIPER
ROBERTS
STRANGE
ANDREWS

MONTHLY TOTALS

| 013 | **5** | Enter the data shown below: | 060 |

	JAN	FEB	MAR	TOTAL NO	UNIT COST
KENT	550	580	650		£3.00
WOODS	600	600	600		£3.50
PIPER	630	630	635		£3.00
ROBERTS	450	475	500		£4.00
STRANGE	650	700	500		£4.00
ANDREWS	510	480	495		£5.00

018	**6**	Use a formula to calculate: **a** the TOTAL NO for each person **b** the AMOUNT (TOTAL NO ★ UNIT COST) **c** MONTHLY TOTALS	
	7	Print your spreadsheet.	062, 063
★019	**8**	Add a heading **APR** after **MAR** and before **TOTAL NO**. Insert the following figures:	

KENT	550	ROBERTS	350
WOODS	450	STRANGE	600
PIPER	570	ANDREWS	490

| ★020 | **9** | Change all **UNIT COSTS** to £6.00, and recalculate the **AMOUNTS**. | |
| | **10** | Save and print the spreadsheet. | 062, 063 |

COMMAND CHECKLIST

Complete the list below, referring to any notes you made while carrying out Tasks 1, 2, 3 and 4. You can then use your list as a reference sheet to complete the tasks that follow.

OBJECTIVE		HOW DO I DO IT?
012	Enter text	_____
013	Enter numeric data	_____
014	Delete entries	_____
015	Replace entries	_____
016	Replicate entries	_____
017	Change the format	_____
018	Use a formula	_____
		_____
		_____
		_____
★019	Add a row Add a column	_____
★020	Project new values	_____
		_____
		_____

You may also wish to make a note of the **default settings** of your spreadsheet program, and other useful commands.

	DEFAULT SETTING
Cell size	_____
Cell format	_____
Fix titles	_____
Print formulae	_____

RSA ASSIGNMENTS & SELF-ASSESSMENTS

TASK 5

WHAT'S THIS TASK FOR?

This task is designed to allow practice of a
complete CLAIT assignment. All the CLAIT
spreadsheet objectives are covered and some of
the CLAIT Section 2 objectives relating to the use of
the system are included.

	1	Power up the system.	056
	2	Load up your spreadsheet program.	057
012	**3**	Enter the heading **HOUSE SALES**	060
012	**4**	Enter the following headings:	060

AGENT HOYLAKE UPTON IRBY CHESTER OXTON COMMISSION AMOUNT

012	**5**	In the first column enter the following titles (left-justified):	060

SMITH & JONES
HALLGATES
BELL & COYNE
GALLAGHERS
SMITH & JOHNS
BOUNDARIES

TOTAL PER AREA

013	**6**	Enter the data shown below:	060

AGENT	HOYLAKE	UPTON	IRBY	CHESTER	OXTON	COM
SMITH & JONES	45	6	56	34	7	4
HALLGATES	12	9	27	51	30	4
BELL & COYNE	19	19	20	15	33	4
GALLAGHERS	27	25	45	22	18	4
SMITH & JOHNS	44	62	38	22	19	4
BOUNDARIES	39	53	31	27	27	4

	7	Save your spreadsheet and print it.	062, 063
	8	There is an error in the data; make the following change:	

      HALLGATES sold **30** houses in **IRBY**

015			
014	**9**	The **CHESTER** entries have been placed in the wrong area; delete the **CHESTER** column.	
017	**10**	The **COMMISSION** figures should be shown as **£4.00**. Change the format of the cells in the **COMMISSION** column to display to 2 decimal places.	
018	**11**	Use a formula to calculate the **TOTAL PER AREA** for **HOYLAKE**.	
016	**12**	Use the replicate command to copy the formula for HOYLAKE and so calculate the **TOTALS** for **UPTON**, **IRBY** and **OXTON.**	
★019	**13**	The spreadsheet would be clearer if the **TOTAL PER AGENT** were displayed. Add a column with a suitable heading before the column showing **COMMISSION**.	
018	**14**	Use a formula to calculate:	

    a the **TOTAL PER AGENT**
    b the **AMOUNT (TOTAL PER AGENT ★ COMMISSION)**

	15	Print these formulae.	062, 063
★020	**16**	The **COMMISSION** rate has been altered to **£5.65**. Make this change and recalculate the **AMOUNTS**.	
	17	Save the spreadsheet.	
	18	Load paper into printer, set to top of form and print the spreadsheet.	061, 062, 063
	19	Close down the system.	059

SELF-ASSESSMENT: TASK 5

DID I DO IT CORRECTLY?

- ○ Entered the headings and numeric data with no more than 3 data entry errors
- ○ Deleted the **CHESTER** column
- ○ Changed the number of houses sold by **HALLGATES** in **IRBY** to **30**
- ○ Replicated the formula entry for **TOTAL PER AREA**
- ○ Changed the format in the **COMMISSION** column to display to 2 decimal places
- ○ Used a formula to calculate **TOTAL PER AGENT**
- ○ Used a formula to calculate the **AMOUNT**
- ○ Added the column **TOTAL PER AGENT**
- ○ Altered the **COMMISSION** rate and re-calculated the totals

If you did this task in two hours or less and have met each of the requirements listed above you should be ready to take the CLAIT spreadsheet assessment.

WHAT'S THIS TASK FOR?

This task, while covering all the CLAIT spreadsheet objectives, is presented in a different format, i.e. the changes are shown on copy, not given by instruction.

012, 013, 016	**1** Load your spreadsheet program. **2** Enter the information below:	057 060

NEW BOOKS

	JUNE	JULY	AUG	SEPT	OCT	TOTAL	AVERAGE COST £
FICTION							
Adventure	8	5	6	7	9		3
Spy Stories	12	10	8	10	11		3
Science Fiction	3	7	2	9	5		3
Travel	2	1	0	1	3		3
REFERENCE							
Computing	5	2	2	1	4		3
Geography	2	4	6	3	2		3
Languages	8	3	5	7	4		3

MONTHLY TOTAL

014, 015, 016, 017, 018	**3** Print the spreadsheet. **4** Make the changes shown below:	062, 063 060

NEW BOOKS

	JUNE	JULY	AUG	SEPT	OCT	TOTAL	AVERAGE COST £
FICTION							
Adventure	8	5	6	7	9		3
Spy Stories	~~12~~6	10	8	10	11		3
Science Fiction	3	7	2	9	5		3
~~Travel~~	~~2~~	~~1~~	~~0~~	~~1~~	~~3~~		~~3~~
REFERENCE							
Computing	5	2	**3**	1	4		3
Geography	2	4	6	3	2		3
Languages	8	3	5	7	4		3

MONTHLY TOTAL

Calculate all these figures

Change these figures to 4.50

	5 Save the spreadsheet and print it out.	062, 063

26

★019, ★020

6   There are further changes. Amend as shown and re-calculate the TOTALS.

NEW BOOKS

	JUNE	JULY	AUG	SEPT	OCT	TOTAL	AVERAGE COST £
FICTION							
Adventure	8	5	6	7	9	35	4.50
Spy Stories	6	10	8	10	11	45	4.50
Science Fiction	3	7	2	9	5	26	4.50
REFERENCE							
Computing	5	2	3	1	4	15	4.50
Geography	2	4	6	3	2	17	4.50
Languages	8	3	5	7	4	27	4.50
MONTHLY TOTAL	32	31	30	37	35	165	

TOTAL EXPENDITURE £

Dance	1	2	0	1	0

*Change the figures in the AVERAGE COST column to £5.50. Enter the heading TOTAL EXPENDITURE £ as shown and calculate this figure (TOTAL No OF BOOKS * AVERAGE COST)*

7   Save the spreadsheet and print it.

062, 063

SELF-ASSESSMENT: TASK 6

DID I DO IT CORRECTLY?

- Entered the headings and numeric data with no more than 3 data entry errors
- Deleted the **TRAVEL** row
- Changed the number of new **SPY STORIES** in **JUNE** to 6 and the new **COMPUTING BOOKS** in **AUGUST** to **3**
- Replicated the formula entry for **MONTHLY TOTAL** and **TOTAL**
- Changed the format in the **AVERAGE COST** column to display to 2 decimal places
- Used a formula to calculate the **MONTHLY TOTAL**
- Used a formula to calculate the **TOTAL**
- Added the row **DANCE**
- Altered the **AVERAGE COST**
- Calculated the **TOTAL EXPENDITURE**

If you did this task in two hours or less and have met each of the requirements listed above you should be ready to take the CLAIT spreadsheet assessment.

3 DATABASES OVERVIEW

WHAT IS A DATABASE?

A database is an organised collection of information. It could be described as an 'electronic filing system'. The information is set up so that it can be updated and recalled as required.

NAME: David James
AGE: 17
SCHOOL: Highdale Sch.
TUTOR: Mr Morgan
SUBJECT1: Maths
SUBJECT2: Info. Tec.

Original data

```
NAME      :DAVID JAMES
SCHOOL    :HIGHDALE SCHOOL
AGE       :17
TUTOR     :MR MORGAN
SUBJECT1:MATHS
SUBJECT2:INFORMATION TECHNOLOGY
-----------------------------------
NAME      :TIM RICHARDS
SCHOOL    :ST JOHNS
AGE       :16
TUTOR     :MRS HINE
SUBJECT1:ENGLISH
SUBJECT2:FRENCH
-----------------------------------
NAME      : IAN WATERHOUSE
SCHOOL    :HARBOURNE SCHOOL
AGE       :18
TUTOR     :MRS WRIGHT
SUBJECT1:BIOLOGY
SUBJECT2:ENGLISH

Continue?
```

FILE	RECORD	FIELD
Each set of related records is called a file. The information is set up in the same format for each item in the collection. The file in the illustration above is a collection of information about students.	Each set of fields is known as a **record**. You can visualise the record by looking at the first card of the original data in the illustration above. It is a complete set of information on DAVID JAMES.	The information on each record is stored under headings known as **fields**. The fields in the example above are Name, School, Age, Tutor, Subject 1, Subject 2.

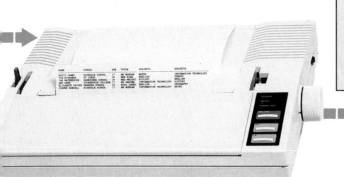

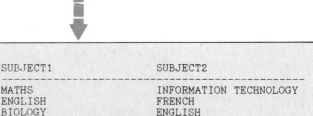

WHY USE A DATABASE?

You can search and sort the information held in a database quickly and accurately. The database program also provides a fast means of finding and retrieving information.

```
NAME              SCHOOL              AGE   TUTOR        SUBJECT1                    SUBJECT2
-----------------------------------------------------------------------------------------------------
DAVID JAMES       HIGHDALE SCHOOL     17    MR MORGAN    MATHS                       INFORMATION TECHNOLOGY
TIM RICHARDS      ST JOHNS            16    MRS HINE     ENGLISH                     FRENCH
IAN WATERHOUSE    HARBOURNE SCHOOL    18    MRS WRIGHT   BIOLOGY                     ENGLISH
AMY DREW          STONEHOUSE COLLEGE  17    MR GROVER    INFORMATION TECHNOLOGY      HISTORY
ELISABETH DAVIES  SWANSEA SCHOOL      16    MISS JONES   ENGLISH                     GEOGRAPHY
JOANNE RANDALL    HIGHDALE SCHOOL     17    MR MORGAN    INFORMATION TECHNOLOGY      MATHS
```

PRINTING DATABASE INFORMATION

Once you have sorted the database or searched it for a particular item of information you may wish to print out that information. You will probably be able to choose whether to print all the information record by record, showing all the fields in each one (see opposite), or whether to produce the information arranged in lists under field headings as above.

You may decide that you do not need to print all the information that the records contain. In this case you would need to decide which fields of the record to print out and then give the appropriate instruction. This would result in printing out 'selected fields'.

```
NAME      :DAVID JAMES
SCHOOL    :HIGHDALE SCHOOL
AGE       :17
TUTOR     :MR MORGAN
SUBJECT1  :MATHS
SUBJECT2  :INFORMATION TECHNOLOGY
--------------------------------
NAME      :TIM RICHARDS
SCHOOL    :ST JOHNS
AGE       :16
```

HOW DATA IS SORTED

There are three different types of fields:

- **Alphabetic:** Only **letters of the alphabet** are recognised by the database. When information is sorted or stored as alphabetic data it is possible to produce alphabetic lists.

- **Numeric:** Only **numbers** are recognised by the database. This allows the records to be sorted in ascending or descending order. On some databases it is also possible to carry out arithmetical tasks.

- **Alphanumeric:** **Letters and numbers** are recognised by the database. The information stored is sorted in alphabetic order.

FINDING THE INFORMATION YOU REQUIRE

SEARCH

During a search the database is interrogated to find a particular item of information. It may look for an 'exact match' or it may simply look for any item which includes a particular word or group of letters.

It is often possible to search on more than one criterion; for example, a database of information on college students and their courses could be searched to find all pupils who are in a particular tutor group AND those who follow an Information Technology course.

SORT

During a sort the records of a database are put into a certain order, e.g. alphabetically in order of surname or in ascending order of height.

DATABASES IN ACTION

Wirral Security Bureau is a firm which has recently bought a computer system and a database program to handle its financial monitoring and finance collection services.

Norman Southern, the company's Managing Director, decided, having taken extensive advice, to install an Amstrad 1512 hard disc system. The program chosen was Delta IV Professional – a transactional database. Hard copy is produced using a dot-matrix printer.

The company has an extensive client list for which it collects and monitors payments.

Norman Southern said:

"At one time we kept all our records on cards. More than one person entered the information about payments and, inevitably, cards were lost or misplaced; moreover, they were not available for use if another member of the staff was using them.

The worst problems occurred when information was not entered on the card and a customer then received a letter of reminder when payment had in fact been made, or when the payment was entered twice which meant that the balance was lower than it should be. It took a great deal of time to rectify the mistake because there was no record of which cards had been used by any particular member of staff.

The new system is a vast improvement. We now have one operator who enters the payments for all our customers. It is possible to view the information quickly if there is a telephone query, and we can monitor the work for the Accounts Department by producing a report of all the payments made that day.

It took a little time to convince the staff that this system could improve our operation. Now, however, they can see the advantages and are all keen to use the system themselves. We are thinking about buying further programs to cover the work in other departments."

BUILD-UP EXERCISES

TASK 1

WHAT'S THIS TASK FOR?

This task is designed to allow you to practise the skills required to gain CLAIT Profile Sentence

P10	Set up a database.

BEFORE YOU BEGIN

You will need to find out and note down how to:

● load your database program.
● set up a file containing alphabetic and numeric fields within the record.

The numbers (e.g. 021) that you see on the left-hand side of the page show the CLAIT database objectives. The numbers that you see on the right-hand side show the CLAIT objectives relating to the use of the system.

	1	Load your database program.	057
021	**2**	Create a data file with the following fields:	

NAME
TOWN
ACCOUNT NO
PRODUCT

022	**3**	Enter the data below:	060

NAME	TOWN	ACCOUNT NO	PRODUCT
WILLIAMS & SON	WIGAN	66155	BOARD
ALUMINA LTD	WIDNES	246831	ENVELOPES
AUSER PACKAGING	ST HELENS	509365	CUT PAPER
BRIZE TRADING	RAMSEY	598357	CUT PAPER
HIGGS & GRIM	SOUTHPORT	301885	BOARD
LITHO SUPPLIES	MAGHULL	583819	ENVELOPES
HURRY PRINT	SOUTHPORT	549266	ALL PAPER
FOCUS	LIVERPOOL	927557	ENVELOPES
MASTERPRINT	WIGAN	66395	ALL PAPER
GERRARD PRINT	PORT ERIN	830118	BOARD

	4	Save and print your file.	062, 063

TASK 2

WHAT'S THIS TASK FOR?

This task is designed to allow you to practise the skills required to gain CLAIT Profile Sentence

| P11 | Enter data and edit a database. |

BEFORE YOU BEGIN

You will need to find out and note down how to:

- enter data.
- add records.
- delete records.
- edit records.

	1	Load your data file from Task 1.	058
022, 023	**2**	Add the following record to your file:	060

NAME	TOWN	ACCOUNT NO	PRODUCT
ALFREDA PLATT	**WIGAN**	**4833758**	**ALL PAPER**

024	**3**	Delete the record of **LITHO SUPPLIES** from your file.	060
025	**4**	Make the following changes to your file:	060
		a the **ACCOUNT NO** of **HURRY PRINT** has changed to **473387**	
		b **FOCUS** have moved to **SOUTHPORT**	
		c the **MASTERPRINT ACCOUNT NO** should be **664395**	
	5	Save your file and print it.	062, 063

TASK 3

WHAT'S THIS TASK FOR?

This task is designed to allow you to practise the skills required to gain CLAIT Profile Sentence

| P12 | Formulate selection procedures for target records. |

BEFORE YOU BEGIN

You will need to find out and note down how to:

- sort records by a keyfield.
- search records by a keyfield.

	1	Load your data file from Task 2.	058
026	**2**	Sort your file by **NAME** into alphabetical order.	
	3	Print your file.	062, 063
027	**4**	Search your file for all those who require **ENVELOPES**, and print the list.	062, 063

TASK 4

WHAT'S THIS TASK FOR?

This task is designed to allow you to practise the skills required to gain CLAIT Profile Sentences

| P13 | Print selected fields. |
| P14 | Search on more than one criterion. |

BEFORE YOU BEGIN

You will need to find out and note down how to:

- print selected fields.
- search on more than one criterion.

	1	Load your data file from Task 3.	058
026	**2**	Sort your file into numerical order using the field headed **ACCOUNT NO.**	
★028	**3**	Print the file, using **ONLY** the following fields:	062, 063
		NAME **ACCOUNT NO**	
★029, ★028	**4**	Search your file for those customers in **WIDNES** who buy **ENVELOPES**, and print the records showing **ONLY**	062, 063
		NAME **ACCOUNT NO**	
	5	Delete your file.	067
	6	Close down the system.	059

COMMAND CHECKLIST

Complete the list below, referring to any notes you made while carrying out Tasks 1, 2, 3, and 4. You can then use your list as a reference sheet to complete the tasks that follow.

OBJECTIVE	HOW DO I DO IT?
021 Set up files containing alphabetic and numeric fields within the record	_____
022 Enter data	_____
023 Add records	_____
024 Delete records	_____
025 Edit records	_____
026 Sort records by a keyfield	_____
027 Search records by a keyfield	_____
028 Print selected fields	_____
029 Search on more than one criterion	_____

You may wish to make a note of other things you need to remember about how your package operates, e.g. any limitations on field length and/or type.

_____ _____

_____ _____

_____ _____

_____ _____

_____ _____

RSA ASSIGNMENTS & SELF-ASSESSMENTS

TASK 5

WHAT'S THIS TASK FOR?

This task is to allow practice of a complete CLAIT
assignment. All the CLAIT database objectives are
covered and some of the CLAIT objectives referring
to the use of the system are included.

021	1	Power up the system and load your database program.	056, 057
	2	Refer to the data to be used and create a file containing the following fields (suitable abbreviations may be used):	

FIELD TITLE	KEY
MAKE	HONDA OR FORD
TYPE	S = SALOON E = ESTATE HB = HATCHBACK
REG NO	
COLOUR	
LOCATION	W = WALLASEY C = CHESTER M = MANCHESTER
YEAR	

022	3 Enter the following details:	060

MAKE	TYPE	REG NO	COLOUR	LOCATION	YEAR
FORD	SALOON	C297 EMH	YELLOW	MANCHESTER	1986
	HATCHBACK	B962 EPK	RED	CHESTER	1984
	SALOON	A493 ERH	RED	CHESTER	1984
	SALOON	A296 NCT	RED	CHESTER	1984
	HATCHBACK	A385 RHV	RED	CHESTER	1984
	ESTATE	B392 RLX	BLUE	WALLASEY	1985
	ESTATE	A392 RPC	GREEN	WALLASEY	1984
	HATCHBACK	B492 RTH	RED	MANCHESTER	1985
	HATCHBACK	A386 UWN	BLUE	MANCHESTER	1984
	ESTATE	B491 WPN	RED	CHESTER	1985
HONDA	SALOON	C297 BDJ	YELLOW	WALLASEY	1985
	HATCHBACK	B219 ERK	GREEN	WALLASEY	1985
	SALOON	B302 FNG	BLUE	CHESTER	1985
	ESTATE	C298 FQO	YELLOW	MANCHESTER	1985
	SALOON	C295 GHW	GREEN	MANCHESTER	1986
	ESTATE	A299 JDN	RED	CHESTER	1984
	SALOON	A976 PKN	BLUE	MANCHESTER	1984
	HATCHBACK	C622 WPB	GREEN	CHESTER	1986

| 023 | 4 | Save your file, load paper into the printer, set to top of form and print your file. | 061, 062, 063 |
| | 5 | Re-load your file, and add the following car to the list: | |

MAKE	TYPE	REG NO	COLOUR	LOCATION	YEAR
HONDA	**SALOON**	**C826 BUR**	**RED**	**WALLASEY**	**1986**

024 6 One of the cars has been sold, delete it from your file:

FORD HATCHBACK   A385 RHV

025 7 Some of the details have been entered incorrectly; make these alterations:

  a the **FORD SALOON A493 ERH** is located in **WALLASEY**
  b the **HONDA ESTATE C298 FQO** is **RED**

026	8	Sort the records by **TYPE**, and print the file.	062, 063
027	9	Re-load your file and search for all the vehicles in **MANCHESTER**. Print the list.	062, 063
★029	10	Search your file for all the **RED FORDS** in **CHESTER**.	
★028	11	Print the list of **RED FORDS** in **CHESTER** showing ONLY the **MAKE, TYPE** and **REG NO.**	062, 063
	12	Delete your file.	067
	13	List your directory to ensure that the files have been erased.	066
	14	Close down the system.	059

SELF-ASSESSMENT: TASK 5

DID I DO IT CORRECTLY?

- ○ Set up files containing alphabetic and numeric fields within the record
- ○ Entered the data with no more than 3 data entry errors
- ○ Added the record for the HONDA SALOON
- ○ Deleted the record for the FORD HATCHBACK
- ○ Edited the record for the FORD SALOON
- ○ Edited the record for the HONDA ESTATE
- ○ Sorted the file by TYPE
- ○ Searched the file for all vehicles in MANCHESTER
- ○ Searched for all the RED FORDS in CHESTER
- ○ Printed the RED FORDS in CHESTER showing only MAKE, TYPE and REG NO

If you did this task in two hours or less and have met each of the requirements listed above you should be ready to take the CLAIT database assessment.

TASK 6

WHAT'S THIS TASK FOR?

This task, while covering all the CLAIT database
objectives, is presented in a different format, i.e. the
changes are shown on copy, not given by
instruction.

	1	Power up the system and load your database program.	056, 057
021	**2**	Refer to the data to be used and create a file containing the following fields (suitable abbreviations may be used):	

<u>FIELD TITLE</u>	<u>KEY</u>
PUBLICATION	
DATE SOLD	DAY (IN FIGURES) OR DAILY
COST OF A4 ADVERT	
COST OF A5 ADVERT	
CIRCULATION	
AREA	N = NORTH S = SOUTH
TYPE	NP = NEWSPAPER TP = TRADE PAPER HP = HOUSE PAPER

022   **3**   Enter the following details: 060

TYPE PUBLICATION	DATE	COST A4	COST A5	CIRC	AREA
TRADE					
AUCTION WORLD	28	120.00	65.00	14500	**N**
HERALDS	1	40.00	25.00	12000	**S**
PLAN IT	1	250.00	125.00	30000	**S**
RACE NEWS	2	100.00	60.00	150000	**S**
RACER	22	50.00	30.00	6000	**S**
RECORDS	21	250.00	130.00	20000	**S**
SEW WHAT	18	120.00	65.00	10000	**N**
HOUSE					
AIRPOL	28	75.00	40.00	25000	**S**
ENTERTAINERS	27	40.00	20.00	3000	**S**
GRAPES	1	200.00	120.00	50000	**N**
IN-STREAM	15	45.00	25.00	5000	**N**
SCOPE	28	150.00	80.00	8500	**N**
DAILY NEWSPAPERS					
DAILY COURIER		150.00	80.00	20000	**N**
DAILY GLOBE		200.00	120.00	200000	**N**
DAILY JOURNAL		300.00	160.00	350000	**S**
DAILY NEWS		50.00	30.00	6000	**N**
EVENING STAR		120.00	65.00	40000	**S**
LOCAL GAZETTE		60.00	35.00	7500	**N**

026

025

4   Sort your file into alphabetical order, then save and print it.

062, 063

5   Make the alterations shown below:

PUBLICATION	DATE	COST A4	COST A5	CIRC	AREA	TYPE
AIRPOL	28	75.00	40.00	25000	S	HP
AUCTION WORLD	28	120.00	65.00	14500	N	TP
DAILY COURIER	DAILY	150.00	80.00	/20000	N	NP
DAILY GLOBE	DAILY	200.00	120.00	200000	N	NP
DAILY JOURNAL	DAILY	300.00	160.00	350000	S	NP
~~DAILY NEWS~~	~~DAILY~~	~~50.00~~	~~30.00~~	~~6000~~	~~N~~	~~NP~~
ENTERTAINERS	27	40.00	20.00	3000	S	HP
~~EVENING STAR~~	~~DAILY~~	~~120.00~~	~~65.00~~	~~40000~~	~~S~~	~~NP~~
GRAPES	1	200.00	120.00	50000	N	HP
HERALDS	1	40.00	25.00	12000	S	TP
IN-STREAM	15	45.00	25.00	5000	N	HP
LOCAL GAZETTE	~~DAILY~~ /6	60.00	35.00	7500	N	~~T~~P
PLAN IT	1	250.00	125.00	30000	S	TP
RACE NEWS	2	100.00	60.00	150000	S	TP
RACER	22	50.00	30.00	6000	S	TP
RECORDS	21	250.00	130.00	20000	S	TP
SCOPE	28	150.00	80.00	8500	N	HP
SEW WHAT	18	120.00	65.00	10000	N	TP

023

ADD THE FOLLOWING RECORDS:

DAILY STAR	DAILY	180.00	100.00	100000	N	NP
BOLT ON	10	75.00	40.00	7500	N	TP

027

6   Search for all the **DAILY PUBLICATIONS**, and print the list.

062, 063

★029, ★028

7   Re-load your file and search for all those **TRADE PAPERS** published in the **NORTH**. Print these records showing ONLY:

062, 063

PUBLICATION DATE COST A4 COST A5 CIRCULATION

8   Delete your file.

067

9   List your directory to ensure that the files have been erased.

066

10   Close down the system.

059

SELF-ASSESSMENT: TASK 6

DID I DO IT CORRECTLY?

- ○ Set up files containing alphabetic and numeric fields within the record
- ○ Entered the data with no more than 3 data entry errors
- ● Added the record for the **DAILY STAR**
- ● Added the record for the **BOLT ON**
- ● Deleted the record for the **DAILY NEWS**
- ● Deleted the record for the **EVENING STAR**
- ● Edited the record for the **DAILY COURIER**
- ● Edited the record for the **LOCAL GAZETTE**
- ● Sorted the file into alphabetical order
- ● Searched the file for all the **DAILY PUBLICATIONS**
- ● Searched for all the **TRADE PAPERS** published in the **NORTH**
- ○ Printed the **trade papers** published in the **north** showing only **PUBLICATION, DATE, COST A4, COST A5, CIRCULATION**

If you did this task in two hours or less and have met each of the requirements listed above you should be ready to take the CLAIT database assessment.

4 VIDEOTEX OVERVIEW

WHAT IS VIDEOTEX?

Videotex is the general name given to information systems which transmit data. Such information systems use television or telephone links, and the information is displayed on computer or television screens. There are two main types of videotex: **TELETEXT** and **VIEWDATA**.

TELETEXT

WHAT IS TELETEXT?

Teletext is a one-way non-interactive system which displays a sequence of screens of information. Teletext is broadcast over the VHF airwaves with normal television signals and it can be received by television sets which have teletext equipment.

CEEFAX

This is the name given to the BBC's teletext service.

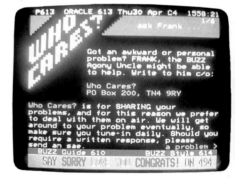

ORACLE

This is the name given to the ITV's teletext service.

VIEWDATA

WHAT IS VIEWDATA?

Viewdata is a two-way interactive information system. A central computer is used to store a variety of information about different topics. Members of the viewdata system connect their computer, via a modem, through the telephone system, to the central computer. Once connected, the subscriber can access the central store of information or use any of the services available. Prestel and TTNS are British examples of viewdata systems.

PRESTEL

British Telecom's Prestel service provides a useful store of information for both domestic and business subscribers. As well as supplying information, the service offers other facilities such as electronic mail, telebanking, teleshopping and telesoftware.

THE TIMES NETWORK SERVICE (TTNS)

This is a viewdata service designed for and used by schools, colleges, etc.

WHY USE VIDEOTEX INFORMATION SYSTEMS?

Videotex systems provide simple and easy methods of displaying information. The screen displays can be composed from a range of coloured text and coloured graphics. The information contained in the system is presented in an organised and structured manner so that it can be retrieved easily.

TREE STRUCTURE OF A VIDEOTEX SYSTEM

A 'tree structure' is the term used to describe how information is stored in a videotex system. The **pages** of information are ordered as shown in the diagram below. When you first call up the system you are given a menu listing the next set of pages available. You then select the number of the page you want, and this moves you on to that page. At this second level you could be given another menu with another set of choices. Having made your selection, you reach a further level. You just repeat this process until you reach the information you require.

The diagram below provides a simplified view of how such a system works. Imagine you were looking for the latest information about British Rail. First you would look at the main menu on level 1 and select **2 TRAVEL**. This would lead to the second page on level 2 where you would select **1 RAIL**. The first page on level 3 offers two choices: latest information and timetables, so you would select **1 LATEST INFORMATION**. This would lead you to the information you required.

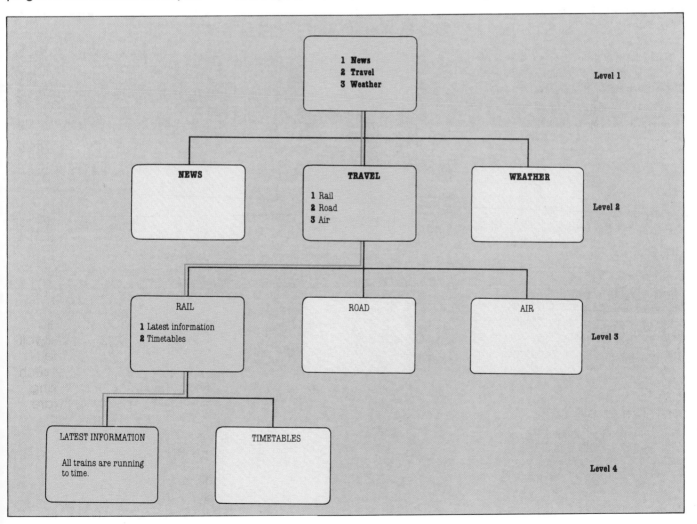

	1 News **2 Travel** **3 Weather**	Level 1
NEWS	**TRAVEL** 1 Rail 2 Road 3 Air	**WEATHER** Level 2
RAIL 1 Latest information 2 Timetables	**ROAD** **AIR**	Level 3
LATEST INFORMATION All trains are running to time.	**TIMETABLES**	Level 4

TECHNIQUES USED TO CREATE TELETEXT PAGES

THE SCREEN DISPLAY

COLOURED TEXT: Teletext systems usually offer seven colours: red, green, blue, magenta, cyan, yellow and white. You will need to decide which make the most attractive display for your information.

BACKGROUND COLOUR: This facility gives variety to your pages. You can make interesting combinations of colour with text and background.

DOUBLE-HEIGHT CHARACTERS: This style is useful for displaying headings. The large characters help make the information stand out more.

FLASHING CHARACTERS: These draw the reader's attention to the screen. It is possible to make a message flash on and off, or change from one colour to another.

GRAPHICS: Some packages let you draw using a cursor drawing facility. With others you have to give special codes to the computer. There is a standard system of codes available. The example below shows how, with a control code, pressing the letters **S A R A** will form the pattern on the screen.

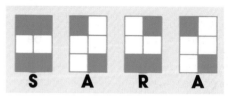

PLANNING SHEETS

If you are not sure how you want your page to look you may wish to use a planning sheet **before** keying in your work.

The planning sheet is carefully divided into the number of lines available across and down the videotex page. The grid will help you plan the exact position of text and graphics on the screen.

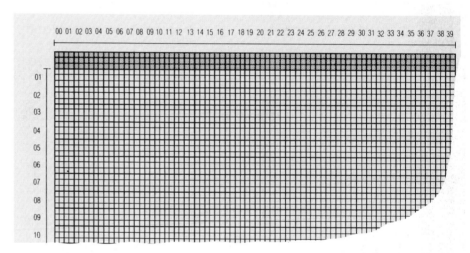

ENTERING YOUR DESIGN

Each teletext package is different, but you will always need to know the codes your package recognises. It is these control codes that allow you to take advantage of what your system offers.

POST EARLY

FOR CHRISTMAS

KEY 0 FOR MAIN MENU

VIDEOTEX IN ACTION

Thomas Cook Ltd is a national network of travel agencies. All the outlets provide the same services for their customers. Travel arrangements can be made by getting advice on the most suitable locations for holidays and information on prices; and customers can confirm those arrangements at the time of booking.

At the agent's site in Liscard, Wallasey, bookings with the travel companies are made using the Prestel system. This allows direct and immediate up-to-date details of the holidays available to be viewed on screen. Decisions can be made there and then on the suitability of the booking, and confirmation received for the customer.

Arrangements can be made not only for international travel, but also for national travel, whether by air, rail, sea or road services.

Travel agents have been using Prestel (viewdata) type programs for some time. Sue Morrison, one of the booking clerks, described its advantages:

" Before we had the use of this system, all the bookings with the travel companies had to be made over the telephone. This meant that you often wasted a lot of time trying to get through to the companies, and it was expensive using the telephone in this way.

It could take many calls before you found a suitable vacancy for the customer and often a good deal of time, too. Now you can get the information much more quickly, and you can also compare different holidays before a decision is made. It means we can provide a better service for the customer. "

A VIDEOTEX SYSTEM

The videotex assignments are designed for use on a local videotex system. The pages of information that follow must be entered for you by someone who knows the system, following the routeing structure given below. You must then go straight to the first assignment on page 47, without looking at the information on the pages in between.

TREE STRUCTURE

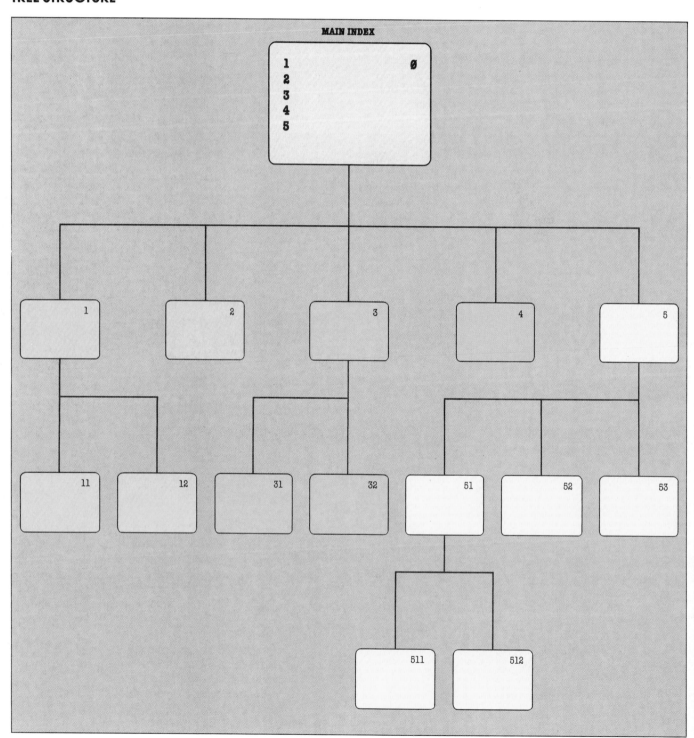

```
              CONTINENTS
          1   EUROPE
          2   ASIA
          3   AFRICA
          4   AUSTRALASIA
          5   AMERICA

      ★ ★ ★   PRESS A NUMBER   ★ ★ ★
```

Page Ø

```
EUROPE
                    1              2
COUNTRY           AUSTRIA        FRANCE
CAPITAL           VIENNA         PARIS
LANGUAGE          GERMAN         FRENCH
CURRENCY          SCHILLING      FRANC

      ★ ★ ★   PRESS Ø FOR MAIN MENU   ★ ★ ★
```

Page 1

```
ASIA
                    1              2
COUNTRY           JAPAN          SAUDI ARABIA
CAPITAL           TOKYO          RIYADH
LANGUAGE          JAPANESE       ARABIC
CURRENCY          YEN            RIYAL

      ★ ★ ★   PRESS Ø FOR MAIN MENU   ★ ★ ★
```

Page 2

```
AFRICA
                    1              2
COUNTRY           TUNISIA        EGYPT
CAPITAL           TUNIS          CAIRO
LANGUAGE          ARABIC/FRENCH  ARABIC
CURRENCY          DINAR          EGYPT £

      ★ ★ ★   PRESS Ø FOR MAIN MENU   ★ ★ ★
```

Page 3

```
AUSTRALASIA
                    1              2
COUNTRY           AUSTRALIA      NEW ZEALAND
CAPITAL           CANBERRA       WELLINGTON
LANGUAGE          ENGLISH        ENGLISH
CURRENCY          AS $           NZ $

      ★ ★ ★   PRESS Ø FOR MAIN MENU   ★ ★ ★
```

Page 4

```
AMERICA

    1        NORTH AMERICA

    2        SOUTH AMERICA

      ★ ★ ★   PRESS Ø FOR MAIN MENU   ★ ★ ★
```

Page 5

```
AUSTRIA

POPULATION                      7,507,000
POPULATION (CAPITAL)            1,587,000
AREA (SQ KM)                       84,000
DENSITY                                89

      ★ ★ ★   PRESS Ø FOR MAIN MENU   ★ ★ ★
```

Page 11

```
FRANCE

POPULATION                     53,788,000
POPULATION (CAPITAL)            9,863,000
AREA (SQ KM)                      547,000
DENSITY                              98.3

      ★ ★ ★   PRESS Ø FOR MAIN MENU   ★ ★ ★
```

Page 12

TUNISIA

POPULATION	6,363,000
POPULATION (CAPITAL)	944,000
AREA (SQ KM)	164,000
DENSITY	38.8

★ ★ ★   PRESS Ø FOR MAIN MENU   ★ ★ ★

Page 31

EGYPT

POPULATION	41,995,000
POPULATION (CAPITAL)	5,084,000
AREA (SQ KM)	1,001,000
DENSITY	42.0

★ ★ ★   PRESS Ø FOR MAIN MENU   ★ ★ ★

Page 32

NORTH AMERICA

	1	2
COUNTRY	UNITED STATES OF AMERICA	CANADA
CAPITAL	WASHINGTON	OTTOWA
LANGUAGE	ENGLISH	ENGLISH/FRENCH
CURRENCY	$	CAN $

★ ★ ★   PRESS Ø FOR MAIN MENU   ★ ★ ★

Page 51

SOUTH AMERICA

	1	2
COUNTRY	CHILE	BRAZIL
CAPITAL	SANTIAGO	BRASILIA
LANGUAGE	SPANISH	PORTUGUESE
CURRENCY	PESO	CRUZEIRO

★ ★ ★   PRESS Ø FOR MAIN MENU   ★ ★ ★

Page 52

★ ★ ★   PRESS Ø FOR MAIN MENU   ★ ★ ★

Page 53

UNITED STATES OF AMERICA

POPULATION	227,640,000
POPULATION (CAPITAL)	3,021,000
AREA (SQ KM)	9,363,000
DENSITY	24.3

★ ★ ★   PRESS Ø FOR MAIN MENU   ★ ★ ★

Page 511

CANADA

POPULATION	23,941,000
POPULATION (CAPITAL)	693,000
AREA (SQ KM)	9,976,000
DENSITY	2.4

★ ★ ★   PRESS Ø FOR MAIN MENU   ★ ★ ★

Page 512

BUILD-UP EXERCISES

TASK 1

WHAT'S THIS TASK FOR?

This task is designed to allow you to practise the skills required to gain CLAIT Profile Sentences

P15	Log on to a videotex system.
P16	Trace pages on a specific topic.

BEFORE YOU BEGIN

You will need to find out and note down how to:

- log on to a viewdata and/or teletext system.
- trace pages on a specific topic.

The numbers (e.g. 030) that you see on the left-hand side of the page show the CLAIT videotex objectives. The numbers on the right-hand side show the CLAIT objectives relating to the use of the system.

030	**1**	Log on to your viewdata system.	056
031	**2**	Go to page 4 and write down the **CAPITAL** of **NEW ZEALAND**.	
031	**3**	Go to page 11 and write down the **AREA** and **DENSITY** of **AUSTRIA**.	
031	**4**	Go to page 32 and write down the **POPULATION** of the **CAPITAL** of **EGYPT**.	
031	**5**	Go to page 511 and write down the **POPULATION** of the **UNITED STATES OF AMERICA**.	

TASK 2

WHAT'S THIS TASK FOR?

This task is designed to allow you to practise the skills required to gain CLAIT Profile Sentences

P17	Amend a directory of pages available.
P18	Edit a page.
P19	Change the routeing of a page.

BEFORE YOU BEGIN

You will need to find out and note down how to:

- amend a directory of pages.
- edit a page.
- change the routeing of a page.

030	**1**	Log on to your viewdata system.
032	**2**	Add the following to page 5:
		3 THE CARIBBEAN
034	**3**	Interchange the routeing of pages 51 and 52.
033	**4**	Edit page 5 to correspond with the changes in step 3.
	5	Save your file.

TASK 3

WHAT'S THIS TASK FOR?

This task is designed to allow you to practise the skills required to gain CLAIT Profile Sentence

P20	Compose a new page using a variety of techniques.

BEFORE YOU BEGIN

You will need to find out and note down how to:

- use coloured text.
- use double-height characters.
- display text flashing.
- use graphics.
- use background filling.

030
★035, ★036, ★037,
★038, ★039

1 Log on to your viewdata system.
2 Compose a new page (53) using:

a double-height characters for the main heading, followed by graphics
b coloured text for the headings COUNTRY, CAPITAL, LANGUAGE and CURRENCY
c flashing for the numbers **1** and **2**
d background filling.

060

```
THE CARIBBEAN


                          1                      2

    COUNTRY           JAMAICA              BARBADOS
    CAPITAL           KINGSTON             BRIDGETOWN
    LANGUAGE          ENGLISH/CREOLE       ENGLISH
    CURRENCY          JAM $                BARB $



         ★★★   PRESS Ø FOR MAIN MENU   ★★★
```

3 Save your page and print it.
4 Close down the system.

062, 063
059

COMMAND CHECKLIST

Complete the list below, referring to any notes you made while carrying out Tasks 1, 2 and 3. You can then use your list as a reference sheet to complete the tasks that follow.

OBJECTIVE	HOW DO I DO IT?
030 Log on to a viewdata and/or teletext system	_____
031 Trace pages on a specific topic	_____
032 Amend a directory of pages available	_____
033 Edit a page	_____
034 Change the routeing of a page	_____

Compose a new page using techniques of:

★035 coloured text	_____
★036 double-height characters	_____
★037 flashing	_____
★038 graphics	_____
★039 background filling	_____

RSA ASSIGNMENTS & SELF-ASSESSMENTS

TASK 4

WHAT'S THIS TASK FOR?

This task is designed to allow practice of a
complete CLAIT assignment. All the CLAIT videotex
objectives are covered and some of the CLAIT
objectives referring to the use of the system are
included.

030	**1** Log on to your viewdata system.	
031	**2** Find out the following information and write down your answers on the **Task 4 answer sheet**:	060
	a What is the **POPULATION** of the **CAPITAL CITY** of **AUSTRIA**?	
	b What is the **CURRENCY** used in the **SOUTH AMERICAN COUNTRY** of **BRAZIL**?	
032	**3** Add the following to page 5: **3 CENTRAL AMERICA**	
034	**4** Interchange the routeing of pages 31 and 32.	
033	**5** Edit page 3 to correspond with the changes in step 4.	
	6 Using the text below, compose a new page (53) using:	
★036, ★038	**a** double-height characters for the main heading, followed by graphics	
★035	**b** coloured text for the headings **COUNTRY, CAPITAL, LANGUAGE** and **CURRENCY**,	
★037, ★039	**c** flashing for the numbers **1** and **2**	
	d background filling	

```
CENTRAL AMERICA


                        1                    2


COUNTRY         CUBA                 COSTA RICA
CAPITAL         HAVANA               SAN JOSE
LANGUAGE        SPANISH/ENGLISH      SPANISH
CURRENCY        PESO                 COLON



        ★★★  PRESS Ø FOR MAIN MENU  ★★★
```

	7 Save your file, load paper into printer, set paper and printer to top of form and print your page.	061, 062, 063,
	8 Close down the system.	059

A copy of the following sheet must be
completed if you are attempting Task 4.

TASK 4 ANSWER SHEET

2 **a** What is the POPULATION of the **CAPITAL CITY** of **AUSTRIA?**

   _____

   b What is the **CURRENCY** used in the **SOUTH AMERICAN COUNTRY** of **BRAZIL?**

   _____

SELF-ASSESSMENT: TASK 4

DID I DO IT CORRECTLY?

- Logged on to a viewdata and/or teletext system
- Found out the population of the **CAPITAL CITY** of **AUSTRIA**
- Found out the **CURRENCY** used in **BRAZIL**
- Added the information to page 5
- Interchanged the routeing of pages 31 and 32
- Edited page 3 to correspond to the routeing change

Composed a new page using techniques of:
- coloured text
- double-height characters
- flashing characters
- graphics
- background filling

If you did this task in two hours or less and have met
each of the requirements listed above you should
be ready to take the CLAIT videotex assessment.

TASK 5

WHAT'S THIS TASK FOR?

This task is designed to allow practice of a
complete CLAIT assignment. All the CLAIT videotex
objectives are covered and some of the CLAIT
objectives referring to the use of the system are
included.

030	**1** Log on to your viewdata system.	
031	**2** Find out the following information and write down your answers on the **Task 5 answer sheet**:	060
	a What is the **AREA (SQ KM)** of **CANADA**?	
	b What **LANGUAGES** do the people speak in **TUNISIA**?	
032	**3** Add the following to page 5:	
	3 CENTRAL AMERICA	
034	**4** Interchange the routeing of pages 31 and 32.	
033	**5** Edit page 3 to correspond with the changes in step 4.	
	6 Using the text below compose a new page (53) using the following techniques where you consider they are appropriate:	
★035, ★036, ★037 ★038 ★039	**a** double-height characters	
	b coloured text	
	c flashing	
	d background filling	
	e graphics	

```
CENTRAL AMERICA


                              1                    2


        COUNTRY        BAHAMAS            HONDURAS
        CAPITAL        NASSAU             TEGUCIGALPA
        LANGUAGE       ENGLISH            SPANISH
        CURRENCY       BAH $              LEMPIRA


              ★★★   PRESS Ø FOR MAIN MENU   ★★★
```

7 Save your file, load paper into printer, set paper and printer to top of form and print your page.	061, 062, 063
8 Close down the system.	059

A copy of the following sheet must be
completed if you are attempting Task 5.

TASK 5 ANSWER SHEET

2   a   What is the **AREA (SQ KM)** of **CANADA?**

_____

    b   What **LANGUAGES** do people speak in **TUNISIA?**

_____

SELF-ASSESSMENT: TASK 5

DID I DO IT CORRECTLY?

- Logged on to a viewdata and/or teletext system
- Found out the **AREA** of **CANADA**
- Found out the **LANGUAGES** spoken in **TUNISIA**
- Added the information to page 5
- Interchanged the routeing of pages 31 and 32
- Edited page 3 to correspond to the routeing change

Composed a new page using techniques of:
- coloured text
- double-height characters
- flashing characters
- graphics
- background filling

If you did this task in two hours or less and have met
each of the requirements listed above you should
be ready to take the CLAIT videotex assessment.

5 BUSINESS/ACCOUNTING
OVERVIEW

WHAT ARE THE MAIN BUSINESS/ ACCOUNTING PACKAGES?

Business and accounting packages are programs which allow computers to store and organise data on a particular aspect of business. There are many examples of such programs. The most common are for **stock control**, **payroll** and the upkeep of various ledger accounts such as the **general ledger, sales ledger** and **purchase ledger.**

PAYROLL

INPUT

The original data is collected by the method most suited to the company or business. It may come from the employee or from external sources. Then the information is keyed into the computer and stored under headings such as:

- Employee's name
- Gross pay to date
- NHI code
- Hourly rate of pay
- Total tax to date
- Employer's NI to date
- Tax code
- Overtime rate
- Employee's NI to date

The program is usually menu-driven so that the operator can easily select the option required.

PROCESS

The information that has been entered may be changed or amended. For instance, it will be possible for changes in tax codes or pay rates to be entered. The program will also allow the details of new employees to be added and the details of past employees to be removed. Once the necessary details have been keyed in, the employees' wages will be calculated.

OUTPUT

When the information has been entered it can be looked at in different ways, and either displayed on screen or printed out as hard copy. The printouts may be in the form of individual pay slips for employees, a pay list of all employees or listings of specified information.

MEMO

To: Wages and Salaries Manager
From: Personnel Director

Annual salary review

Following the meeting of the Board of Directors yesterday, I can now confirm an increase of 5 per cent on all salaries to be effective from 1 January.

➡ PROCESS ➡

Tax Code	242L	31 JAN 88
Contribution letter	D	
N.I. No	NA000000A	HARVEY MRS KJ

Pay and allowances		Deductions	
Basic Pay	868.75	Income Tax	180.00
		Nat. Insurance	78.19
		Total	258.19
Total	868.75	Net Pay	610.56

WHY USE BUSINESS/ACCOUNTING PACKAGES?

Such packages are used because they are specially designed for the job in hand. The program will have been written to store a certain type of data, to organise and process that data in the most suitable manner, and to perform any calculations on it that may be required.

STOCK CONTROL

INPUT

The information that is required to run a stock control system efficiently will come from several sources: invoices, catalogues, stock sheets and from warehouse records. Such information will be keyed in and stored under headings such as:

- Description of goods
- Cost price
- Units in stock
- Name of supplier
- Unit quantity
- Selling price
- Minimum stock level/re-order quantity
- Address of supplier

PROCESS

The information that is held in the package can be edited and updated. The products in stock may vary or the suppliers of a product may change. It is also possible to search the system for a particular item to check if it is in stock. When new products are introduced these can be added to the stock lists and products no longer stocked can be deleted. Most stock control programs will automatically calculate the value of stock, both for individual items and the complete stock held.

OUTPUT

Information on the products can be checked on the screen. It is also possible to produce printed lists of all stocks held, goods required for ordering, price lists, and other specified information. The information on items that have fallen below their stock re-order levels will be of particular importance to a business and some stock control programs will not only display this information when requested but also print out the letter which re-orders the goods.

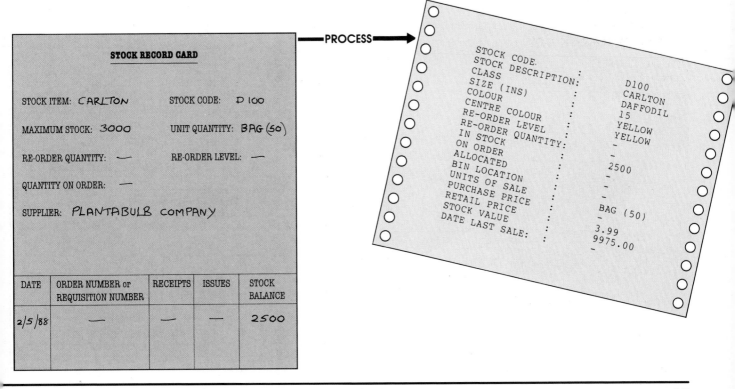

PAYROLL IN ACTION

E.J. Horrocks (Wirral) & Co Ltd is a builders' merchants whose head office is in Birkenhead on the Wirral, with another site in Winsford, Cheshire.

The company has been in operation for over twenty-five years, and since the early 1980s, some of the company's business has been carried out using a computer.

Ted Horrocks, Managing Director, made the decision to upgrade the system in order to computerise the entire operation. He chose the Research Machines Nimbus network so that he would be able to communicate with the other office.

Most of the programs he required were available 'off-the-shelf', but in some instances amendments had to be made to the software so that it suited the building trade.

Ted Horrocks explained:

We had been using a computer for some time when we introduced the new system. In some cases staff had to be re-trained before they could use the new programs. They were able to help in the planning of the new installation, as they were aware of the day-to-day requirements in this industry.

This was particularly true of the payroll program, because there are some specialities in the system used by the building trade which would not have been included in a standard payroll program.

Rob Armstrong, who operates the network for the company, added:

The new system uses fully integrated software and therefore we are able to cut back on the amount of data that we have to enter into the computer. Now that the software house has made the amendments to suit our specific requirements, we find that the whole operation runs much more smoothly, and takes less operator time.

STOCK CONTROL IN ACTION

James Edwards (Chester) Ltd is a member of the Allied Lyons Group. It is the head office for seven other garages in the North West region.

The office has a BTI8000 series mini-computer. Its facilities cover all the needs of all the departments at the Chester branch, and it has on-line communication, via modems, not only to the other sites, but also to the stock control division of the manufacturers at Longbridge.

Nick Cook, Group Accountant, talked enthusiastically about the computer installation:

We have recently upgraded the system, and we now find that we are able to run the whole operation more smoothly. We have also been able to cut deadlines back dramatically. We send information via the modems overnight. This cuts back on costs and is more efficient and so we can pass on these savings to our customers.

The stock control in the Parts Department is one of the areas that has been improved. We are able to monitor the whole system far more effectively. The parts are ordered from the factory across the computer network and, using the system, their arrival is much faster. On arrival the parts are logged into the system.

If anyone requires a particular part they can check very quickly whether or not we have it in stock. If some of these parts are then withdrawn from stock, the program reduces the stock figure by the number that have been withdrawn and invoices the department that has removed them.

This new system has meant that we are able to deal far more effectively with our work. It cuts down on the waiting time for parts – particularly in the workshops, where it is not productive to have vehicles off the road for any longer than necessary.

COMMAND CHECKLIST : PAYROLL

Complete the list below, referring to any notes you may have. You can then use your list as a reference sheet to complete the tasks that follow.

OBJECTIVE		HOW DO I DO IT?
040	Enter a variety of business information relevant to the package	_____
041	Search the package for information	_____
042	Add records	_____
043	Delete records	_____
044	Change records	_____
*045	Produce a report on specified information	_____

You may also wish to make a note of other things you need to remember about how your payroll package operates.

_____ _____

_____ _____

_____ _____

_____ _____

_____ _____

_____ _____

RSA ASSIGNMENTS & SELF-ASSESSMENTS : PAYROLL

WHAT'S THIS TASK FOR?

This task is designed to allow practice of a
complete CLAIT assignment. All the CLAIT payroll
objectives are covered and some CLAIT Section 2
objectives relating to the use of the system are
included.

	1	Power up the system and load your payroll program.	056, 057
040	**2**	Refer to the **DETAILS OF WEEKLY PAID EMPLOYEES** sheet that follows and enter the details, together with whatever initial detail is required by your package.	060
040	**3**	Refer to the **TIME SHEET** that follows and enter the details provided for the hours worked in week 35.	
	4	Print out a pay slip for each employee.	062, 063
	5	At the start of week 36:	
044	**a**	**MISS P WILLIAMS** has just married. Recall your file and alter her name to **MRS P OLIVER**	058
043	**b**	**MR J BARNES (0006)** has resigned. Delete his record from the file.	
042	**c**	**MR D COFFEE** joined the company. He has not worked before. Add his record to the file:	

HOURLY RATE	OVERTIME RATE	TAX CODE	NHI STATUS	EMPLOYEE NO	NORMAL HOURS	O'TIME HOURS
£2.95	£4.43	242L	A	0010	35 $\frac{1}{2}$	—

041	**6**	Search for anyone earning **less than £100 gross** in week 36. Print their details.	062, 063
★045	**7**	Load paper into printer, set to top of form and print out a report of all employees' details	061, 062, 063
	8	Save your work and close down the system.	059

STEPHEN TODD ASSOCIATES
DETAILS OF WEEKLY PAID EMPLOYEES

EMPLOYEE NO	0002	0004	0006	0005	0007
Hourly Pay	£2.50	£3.25	£6.25	£4.50	£3.25
Tax Code	379H	379H	242L	379H	242L
Gross Pay to date	£3017.60	£3922.75	£7543.75	£5431.50	£3922.75
Tax to date	£143.90	£388.20	£1607.80	£795.60	£630.10
Overtime Pay (time + half)	£3.33	£4.33	£8.33	£6.00	£4.33
NHI Status	A	A	A	A	A
Employee NI to date	£210.46	£353.26	£677.62	£487.90	£353.26
Employer NI to date	£210.46	£353.26	£787.10	£566.78	£353.26

TIME SHEET		WEEK 35	
NAME	EMPLOYEE NO	NORMAL HOURS WORKED	OVERTIME HOURS
Miss P Williams	0002	35½	—
Mr S Barnes	0004	35½	2
Mr J Barnes	0006	35½	6
Mr P O'Loughlin	0005	35½	2
Miss L Dyer	0007	35½	2

TIME SHEET		WEEK 36	
NAME	EMPLOYEE NO	NORMAL HOURS WORKED	OVERTIME HOURS
Mrs P Oliver	0002	35½	—
Mr S Barnes	0004	35½	2
Mr P O'houghlin	0005	35½	2
Miss L Dyer	0007	35½	2
Mr D Coffee	0010	35½	—

SELF-ASSESSMENT: TASK 1

DID I DO IT CORRECTLY?

○ Entered the **DETAILS OF WEEKLY PAID EMPLOYEES** with no more than 3 data entry errors	○ Added the record for **MR D COFFEE**
	○ Deleted the record for **MR J BARNES**
○ Searched the details for anyone earning less than £100 gross in week 36	○ Changed the record for **MISS P WILLIAMS**
	○ Produced a report of all employees' details

If you did this task in two hours or less and have met each of the requirements listed above you should be ready to take the CLAIT business/accounting assessment.

TASK 2

WHAT'S THIS TASK FOR?

This task is designed to allow practice of a complete CLAIT assignment. All the CLAIT payroll objectives are covered and some CLAIT Section 2 objectives relating to the use of the system are included.

	1	Power up the system and load your payroll program.	056, 057
	2	Load your file from Task 1.	058
040	**3**	Refer to the **TIME SHEET** that follows and enter the details provided for hours worked in week 37.	
	4	Print out a pay slip for each employee.	062, 063
043	**5**	**MISS DYER (0007)** has resigned. Delete her record from the file.	
044	**6**	Refer to the memo from the Managing Director and take the appropriate action.	
042	**7**	**MR D KING** has joined the company. He has not worked before. Add his record to the file:	

HOURLY RATE	TAX CODE	OVERTIME RATE	NHI STATUS	EMPLOYEE NO
3.41	379H	5.12	A	0011

041	**8**	Search for anyone who worked overtime in week 37. Print the details.	062, 063
★045	**9**	Print out a pay list for all employees.	062, 063
	10	Save your file and close down the system.	

TIME SHEET		WEEK 37	
NAME	EMPLOYEE NO	NORMAL HOURS WORKED	OVERTIME HOURS
Mrs P Oliver	0002	35½	—
Mr S Barnes	0004	35½	—
Mr P O'Loughlin	0005	35½	4
Mr D Coffee	0010	35½	—
Miss L Dyer	0007	35½	—

MEMO

FROM Managing Director
REF payinc/MD/acc

TO Accounts
DATE xx/xx/88

PAY INCREASE

Following our recent discussions it has been agreed that the rate
of the annual pay rise is to be 5%. Please ensure that this
increase is included in this week's pay.

The new rates will be as follows:

	0002	0004	0010	0005
HOURLY PAY	2.63	3.41	3.10	4.73
OVERTIME PAY	3.95	5.12	4.65	7.10

SELF-ASSESSMENT: TASK 2

DID I DO IT CORRECTLY?

- Entered the details of **HOURS WORKED IN WEEK 37** from the **TIME SHEET**
- Printed out a pay slip for each employee
- Deleted the record for **MISS DYER**
- Changed the records to take account of the 5% pay increase
- Added the record for **MR D KING**
- Searched the file for anyone who worked overtime in week 37
- Printed a pay list of all employees

COMMAND CHECKLIST : STOCK CONTROL

Complete the list below, referring to any notes you may have. You can then use your list as a reference sheet to complete the tasks that follow.

OBJECTIVE	HOW DO I DO IT?
040 Enter a variety of business information relevant to the package	
041 Search the package for information	
042 Add records	
043 Delete records	
044 Change records	
★045 Produce a report on specified information	

You may also wish to make a note of other things you need to remember about how your stock control program operates.

RSA ASSIGNMENTS & SELF-ASSESSMENTS : STOCK CONTROL

TASK 3

WHAT'S THIS TASK FOR?

This task is designed to allow practice of a complete CLAIT assignment. All the CLAIT stock control objectives are covered and some CLAIT Section 2 objectives relating to the use of the system are included.

040	1	Power up the system and load your stock control program.	056, 057
	2	Set up a file to record the wines listed below with whatever initial detail is required by your package. Within the file you will be using the following headings:	060

ITEM NO
CLASS
DESCRIPTION
SIZE CL
RETAIL VALUE (EACH)
NO IN STOCK

040	3	Enter the details below:

```
STOCK CONTROL DATA SHEET

ITEM    CLASS    DESCRIPTION        SIZE      RETAIL      NO IN
NO                                  CL        VALUE       STOCK
                                              (EACH)

C81     C        CLARET             70         3.75       700
C80     B        CLARET             70         5.85       600
C76     A        CLARET             75        10.50       850
C71     C        CLARET             70         3.60       200
C84     A        CLARET             75        12.50       375

R80     C        RIESLING           75         2.95       715
R81     A        RIESLING           75        13.25       245
R84     C        RIESLING           70         3.95       950
R72     A        RIESLING           70        11.25       380
R71     B        RIESLING           70         4.50       670

B70     A        BURGUNDY           75        10.25       785
B71     B        BURGUNDY           75         5.75       975
B82     C        BURGUNDY           70         2.95       235
B76     C        BURGUNDY           70         3.50       850
B79     A        BURGUNDY           70        18.95       290
```

	4	Load paper into the printer, set the paper and printer to the top of form and print the stock list.	061, 062, 063
042	5	Reload your file and add the following items:	058

ITEM NO	CLASS	DESCRIPTION	SIZE CL	RETAIL VALUE	NO IN STOCK
R73	B	RIESLING	70	4.50	650
B75	A	BURGUNDY	70	16.50	700

043	6	The following items have been sold, delete them from your file:	
		a **R80**	
		b **C71**	
044	7	There are alterations due to sales; make the following changes:	
		ITEM NO NO IN STOCK	
		a **R84** **850**	
		b **B76** **500**	
041	8	Search your file for all the **C CLASS** wines and print these items.	062, 063
★045	9	Produce a report of all the items of **70 CL**.	062, 063
	10	Save your file and close down the system.	059

SELF-ASSESSMENT: TASK 3

DID I DO IT CORRECTLY?

- ○ Entered the details from the **STOCK CONTROL DATA SHEET** with no more than 3 data entry errors
- ○ Searched the details for all **CLASS C WINES**
- ○ Added the records for **ITEM NOS R73** and **B75**
- ○ Deleted the record for **ITEM NOS R80** and **C71**
- ○ Changed the record for **ITEM NOS R84** and **B76**
- ○ Produced a report of all items of **70 CL**

If you did this task in two hours or less and have met each of the requirements listed above you should be ready to take the CLAIT business/accounting assessment.

TASK 4

WHAT'S THIS TASK FOR?

This task is designed to allow practice of a complete CLAIT assignment. All the CLAIT stock control objectives are covered and some CLAIT Section 2 objectives relating to the use of the system are included.

	1	Power up the system and load your stock control program.	056, 057
040	2	Set up a file to record the computer cassettes below, with whatever initial detail is required by your package. Within the file you will be using the following headings:	060
		ITEM NO **DESCRIPTION** **RETAIL £** **STOCK LEVEL** **RE-ORDER LEVEL**	

040

060

3 Enter the details below:

```
┌─────────────────────────────────────────────────────────────┐
│  STOCK CONTROL DATA SHEET                                     │
├─────────────────────────────────────────────────────────────┤
│  ITEM      DESCRIPTION        RETAIL    STOCK     RE-ORDER    │
│  NO                           £         LEVEL     LEVEL       │
│                                                               │
│  AM512     FIRELORD           8.99      150       90          │
│  AM624     TARZAN             8.99      200       50          │
│  AM684     PAPER BOY          7.99      100       90          │
│  AM421     MIAMI VICE         8.99       75       90          │
│  AM788     ALIENS             9.99      100       50          │
│  SC546     TRIVIAL PURSUIT   14.99      150       50          │
│  SC445     STREET HAWK        8.99       90       80          │
│  SC428     GREEN BERET        8.99      100       60          │
│  SC315     MONOPOLY           9.99      150       80          │
│  SC981     REVOLUTION         9.99       60       90          │
│  CD118     HIJACK             9.99      100       80          │
│  CD751     GALVAN             8.99       90       50          │
│  CD039     HEARTLAND          9.99      100       75          │
│  CD860     DRUID              7.99       95       60          │
│  CD759     KNIGHT RIDER       8.99       85       75          │
└─────────────────────────────────────────────────────────────┘
```

4 Save your file, load paper into printer, set paper and printer to top of form and print your file.

061, 062, 063

042

5 Reload your file and add the following items:

ITEM NO	DESCRIPTION	RETAIL £	STOCK LEVEL	RE-ORDER LEVEL
AM551	**TEMPEST**	**7.99**	**100**	**50**
SC118	**GALVAN**	**7.99**	**100**	**50**

043

6 Delete the following items from your file:

a   AM684 PAPER BOY

b   CD860 DRUID

044

7 There are errors in the details; make the following changes:

a   the **ITEM NO** for **MIAMI VICE** should be **AM743**

b   the **DESCRIPTION** for **ITEM NO SC981** should be **TOP GUN**

041

8 Search your file for those cassettes with a **RETAIL PRICE** of £7.99, and print these items.

062, 063

★045

9 Produce a report of all the items below **RE-ORDER LEVEL**.

062, 063

10 Save your file and close down the system.

059

SELF-ASSESSMENT: TASK 4

DID I DO IT CORRECTLY?

- ○ Entered the details from the **STOCK CONTROL DATA SHEET** with no more than 3 data entry errors
- ○ Searched the details for cassettes costing £7.99
- ○ Added the records for **ITEM NOS AM551** and **SC118**
- ○ Deleted the records for **ITEM NOS AM684** and **CD860**
- ○ Changed the record for **ITEM NOS AM743** and **SC981**
- ○ Produced a report of all **items below re-order level**

If you did this task in two hours or less and have met each of the requirements listed above you should be ready to take the CLAIT business/accounting assessment.

6 GRAPHICS AND PLOTTING
OVERVIEW

GRAPHICS

WHAT IS A GRAPHICS DRAWING PACKAGE?

A drawing package allows you to design and draw pictures. With most packages you can build outlines or frameworks, produce and store shapes and symbols, fill in shapes and enter text. You can produce many interesting designs and displays for a variety of purposes.

WHY USE A GRAPHICS DRAWING PACKAGE?

A drawing package lets you produce graphic displays using the computer facilities of editing and storage. For example, you may be able to work on part of a design, then save it, and return to the work at a later stage and change it. The package will also allow you to store shapes and reproduce them in different sizes or at a different angle; there is no need to rebuild the shape. The package may even allow you to use colour and patterns to improve your design.

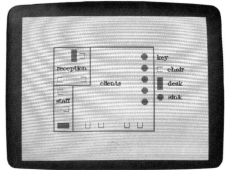

DESIGNS	PLANS	LOGOS

Drawing packages can be used to design drawings for programme covers, advertisements, menus, book jackets, etc. The ability to combine the drawing with text is particularly useful.

Using the facilities of a drawing package it is possible to produce simple maps, office layouts, shop floor layouts, etc. The ability of the computer system to store shapes and reproduce them should make this task much simpler. The edit facilities mean that the design can easily be altered if the information changes.

A logo is a small design used to provide a quick and simple way of identifying a product, school, etc. The program provides a means of designing such a logo, and may be able to produce the logo in a variety of sizes.

GRAPHICAL REPRESENTATION

WHAT IS A GRAPHICAL REPRESENTATION (PLOTTING) PACKAGE?

This is a means of using your computer system to process and then output numerical information in a pictorial form. The information may have been stored by the computer in a database or spreadsheet, or have been specially entered for graphic display. You may then add text as headings or labels to the diagram.

WHY USE A GRAPHICAL REPRESENTATION (PLOTTING) PACKAGE?

Some information can be represented in a much more interesting and eye-catching way using graphics. The computer offers a fast and reliable way of converting the data into this form. You can decide how best to display the information, and even display the same information in several forms.

PRESENTING INFORMATION GRAPHICALLY

There are three main forms of graphical representation of information.

| PIE CHART | HISTOGRAM | LINE GRAPH |

PIE CHART

A pie chart is a useful means of showing how a total is made up of its parts. It consists of a circle cut into a number of segments. Each segment represents a part and is shown as the correct proportion of the circle which represents the total amount. When using a plotting package you need only key in the **actual** value of each part. These are automatically converted into proportions and displayed in pie-chart form.

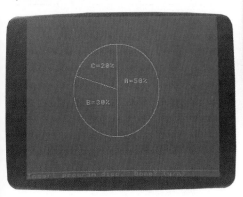

HISTOGRAM

A histogram (or bar chart) uses columns to represent the quantities. It is a useful means of presenting information so that figures charted on the same axis can be compared. Only the values or quantities need to be keyed in. The plotting package automatically produces the columns or bars to the correct size.

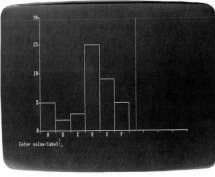

LINE GRAPH

The points on a line graph are plotted with reference to a horizontal and a vertical axis, then a line connecting the points is drawn. With a plotting package the data is entered; then the points are automatically plotted and the connecting line drawn.

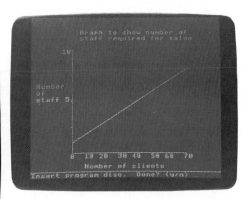

Some plotting packages can represent formulae as line graphs. Such information is often much easier to understand if it is shown graphically. For example the graph on the screen above represents the formula:

$$Y = (X/10) + 1$$

GRAPHIC DESIGN IN ACTION

F. Llewllyn & Co Ltd, based in Liverpool, has long been involved in the manufacturing and supply of equipment for hospitals and Social Services Departments. More recently they have been designing the layout of kitchens for the disabled.

The company uses a Tandon computer. Simon Robson, who operates the computer graphics program used to design the kitchens, explained its advantages:

The program is very versatile and allows changes and adaptations to be made very easily. We are able to design the kitchen with regard to the particular disability of the person concerned.

Firstly we need to enter the dimensions of the room, i.e. the length and the width, plus any other relevant details such as alcoves and storage spaces. We are then able to draw the outline of the room, and we can begin designing the placement of the other items in the kitchen.

If the person for whom the kitchen is being planned is confined to a wheelchair, we have to allow for this in the placing of the units and consider, for example, whether the doors of the units can be opened. It may be that one door must open to the left and another to the right to allow for maximum usage of the room.

The placing of other units must also be carefully considered. It is of little use to place storage cabinets where the client, who may be confined to a wheelchair, is unable to reach them.

We find that using the program allows us maximum flexibility for experimenting with different designs. It also allows us to alter the design easily after consultation with the client. This used to take a great deal more time as the plan had to be completely re-drawn.

GRAPHICAL COMPUTER-AIDED ENGINEERING IN ACTION

The Wirral Computer-Aided Engineering Centre provides a service to local industry and businesses which cannot themselves afford the necessary equipment. The Centre trains their personnel and carries out specific projects. It has departments covering computer-aided design, printed circuit board design and construction, 2D drafting and CNC.

Steve Roberts is responsible for the preparation of work on the lathes and milling machines. He explained:

"Many of the people using our facility have a traditional background in machine turning. The systems we have enable them to program the computer and see a visual display of the finished article. A second advantage is that they can then make alterations quickly and easily to that design.

This is also the case in the drafting department which is involved in the preparation of plans and drawings which would traditionally have been carried out in the drawing office. The advantage of seeing the design graphically and the ease with which amendments and alterations can be made to drawings allows any design to be tried and tested before going to the expense of manufacture. It is also possible for the program to generate cross-sections and alternate views of the design on-screen."

In the PCB design department Peter Whitby described the advantages of the program he uses:

"The program is very easy to use, and it cuts the time needed to prepare even the most complicated boards down to a fraction of the time taken using other methods. You have the advantage of seeing all the detail on screen, and much of the work that would previously have to be carried out manually is now generated by the machine.

Once we have completed the design and we are ready for the next stage, we can even incorporate that design into the manufacturing process. This produces a higher degree of precision than was previously possible."

BUILD-UP EXERCISES

TASK 1

WHAT'S THIS TASK FOR?

This task is designed to allow you to practise the skills required to gain CLAIT Profile Sentence

P25	Draw, change, label and store shapes/symbols.

BEFORE YOU BEGIN

You will need to find out and note down how to:

- load your drawing program.
- draw shapes/symbols.
- change shapes/symbols.
- store shapes/symbols.
- colour sections.
- shade sections.
- use text to label drawings.

The numbers (e.g. 046) that you see on the left-hand side of the page show the CLAIT drawing objectives. The numbers that you see on the right-hand side show the CLAIT Section 2 objectives relating to the use of the system.

046, 050	1 Load your drawing program. 2 Refer to the plan below which shows the outline of the ground floor of a house. Draw the outline as shown on the plan, including the labels; the proportions and scale may differ slightly.	057 060

```
UTILITY ROOM          LOUNGE

                 HALL

KITCHEN        DINING ROOM
```

046, 048	3 The LOUNGE has 2 armchairs, 1 settee and 1 square table. Design the outline shapes for each of these and store them. 4 Position the furniture in the LOUNGE. 5 Print out your plan.	
047 049	6 Replace the square table with a round table. 7 The 2 armchairs and the settee are covered with patterned material. Fill them in with an appropriate pattern. 8 Print out your finished plan.	062, 063 062, 063

TASK 2

WHAT'S THIS TASK FOR?

This task is designed to allow you to practise the skills required to gain CLAIT Profile Sentence

P26	Produce graphical outputs from numeric data.

BEFORE YOU BEGIN

You will need to find out and note down how to:

- produce a pie chart.
- produce a histogram/bar chart.
- produce a graph.
- use text to label graphs/charts.

	1	Load your pie-chart program.	057
051	**2**	Generate a pie-chart using the following values:	060

NORTH	**18**
SOUTH	**22**
MIDLANDS	**33**
SCOTLAND	**27**

054	**3**	Name the chart **AREA SALES PERCENTAGES – JAN TO JUNE**	
054	**4**	Label each segment and add numeric values.	
	5	Print the pie chart.	062, 063
	6	Load your histogram/bar-chart program which you are going to use to display the figures for the **NORTH** for the period **JAN – JUNE.**	057
052, 054	**7**	Name the X (horizontal) axis **MONTHS**, and the Y (vertical) axis **VALUE-£**. Map the steps in appropriate units.	060
	8	Generate a histogram/bar chart using the following values:	

MONTH	VALUE-£
JAN	**12000**
FEB	**20000**
MAR	**22000**
APR	**25000**
MAY	**15000**
JUNE	**10000**

054	**9**	Enter the headings for each month, and title the chart:	

MONTHLY SALES – NORTH

	10	Print your histogram/bar chart.	062, 063
	11	Load and run your graphics program. The subject is Sales Figures for the Southern Region.	057
054	**12**	Name the X (horizontal) axis **MONTHS**, and the Y (vertical) axis **VALUE-£**.	060
053	**13**	Plot the points and generate a line graph from the data given below:	

MONTH	VALUE – £
JAN	**16000**
FEB	**22000**
MAR	**23000**
APR	**28000**
MAY	**20000**
JUNE	**18000**

054	**14**	Title the graph **MONTHLY SALES – SOUTH**. Enter the headings for each month.	
	15	Print your graph.	062, 063

TASK 3

WHAT'S THIS TASK FOR?

This task is designed to allow you to practise the skills required to gain CLAIT Profile Sentence

P27	Use a formula to produce a graph.

BEFORE YOU BEGIN

You will need to find out and note down how to:

⬤ use a formula to produce a graph.

	1	Load your graph program.	057
054	**2**	Name the X (horizontal) axis **POUNDS (LBS)**, and name the Y (vertical) axis **KILOS**.	060
	3	Set the graph to display for:	
		0 to **35 KILOS**	
		0 to **70 POUNDS**	
★055	**4**	Input the formula **Y = X ★ 0.454**, or any other which will relate **POUNDS** to **KILOS**.	
	5	Print out your display.	062, 063

Complete the list below, referring to any notes you may have. You can then use your list as a reference sheet to complete the tasks that follow.

OBJECTIVE		HOW DO I DO IT?
046	Draw shapes/symbols	_____
047	Change shapes/symbols	_____
048	Store shapes/symbols	_____
049	Colour or shade sections	_____
050	Use text to label drawings	_____

Use a variety of prepared data to produce:

051	pie charts	_____
052	histograms	_____
053	graphs	_____
054	Use text to label graphs/charts	_____
★055	Use a formula to produce a graph	_____

You may also wish to make a note of other things you need to remember about how your graphics/ plotting program(s) operate(s).

_____ _____
_____ _____
_____ _____
_____ _____

RSA ASSIGNMENTS & SELF-ASSESSMENTS

TASK 4

WHAT'S THIS TASK FOR?

This task allows you to practise a complete CLAIT assignment. All the CLAIT graphics/plotting objectives are covered and some of the CLAIT objectives relating to the use of the system are included.

PART 1

	1 Power up the system.	056
	2 Load your drawing program.	057
	3 In this part of the assignment you are asked to design the layout of a computer room.	
046, 050	Refer to the plan below which shows the outline of the room. Draw the outline as shown including the labels; proportions and scale may differ slightly.	
046, 048	**4** The room will have 5 rectangular tables; design the outline shape of a table. There will also be 5 chairs. Design the outline shape for the chair and store the shape together with the shape for the table.	060
	5 Position 4 tables in the computer room, and 1 in the office area. The power points are on the walls where shown, so the tables must be placed appropriately. Place a chair by each of the tables.	
	6 Load paper into the printer, set to top of form and print your plan.	061, 062, 063
047	**7** The table in the office area should be square not rectangular. Make this change.	
049	**8** Colour or shade the tables on your plan; use a different colour/pattern for the square table.	
	9 Print your finished plan.	062, 063

PART 2

	1 Load your pie-chart program which is to be used to display the proportion of students who study in the areas shown.	057

051	**2**	Generate a pie chart headed **AREAS OF STUDY** using the values shown below:	060

AREA OF STUDY	NO OF STUDENTS
2D DRAFTING	20
CNC	35
PCB DESIGN	45

054	**3**	Use labels and numeric values for each segment.	
	4	Load the printer with paper and set to top of form; check the printer is on-line and print your pie chart.	061, 062, 063
	5	Load the histogram/bar chart program which is to be used to display the number of participants per course in the CNC department.	057
054	**6**	Name the X (horizontal) axis **COURSE NO**, and the Y (vertical) axis **NO OF PARTICIPANTS**. Map the steps in appropriate units.	060
052, 054	**7**	Generate a histogram/bar chart headed **PARTICIPANTS PER COURSE – CNC** using the following values:	

COURSE NO	NO OF PARTICIPANTS
1	16
2	25
3	18
4	28
5	20
6	19

054	**8**	Label the bars with the COURSE NOS.	
	9	Print your histogram/bar chart.	062, 063
	10	Load your graph program which you will use to display the number of participants per course in the PCB design department.	057
054	**11**	Name the X (horizontal) axis **COURSE NO**, and the Y (vertical) axis **NO OF PARTICIPANTS**. Map the steps in appropriate units.	
053	**12**	Generate a line graph headed **PARTICIPANTS PER COURSE – PCB DESIGN** using the values below:	060

COURSE NO	NO OF PARTICIPANTS
1	26
2	24
3	26
4	28
5	30
6	28

	13	Print your graph.	062, 063
	14	Load your graph program which can use a formula.	057
054	**15**	Name the X (horizontal) axis **CENTIMETRES**, and the Y (vertical) axis **INCHES**.	060
	16	Set the graph to display from:	

    0 to **46 CENTIMETRES**
    0 to **18 INCHES**

★055	**17**	Input the formula $Y = X \star 2.51$ or any other formula which relates **CENTIMETRES** to **INCHES**. Generate your graph headed **CMS/INS conversion**.	
	18	Load the printer with paper and set to top of form, check the printer is on-line and print your display.	061, 062, 063
	19	Close down the system.	059

SELF-ASSESSMENT: TASK 4

DID I DO IT CORRECTLY?

- Drew the outline plan of the room
- Stored the shapes of the table and chair
- Changed the shape of the table
- Coloured or shaded the tables
- Used text to label the drawing as shown

Used a variety of prepared data to produce:
- a pie chart
- a histogram
- a graph
- Used text to label the graphs/charts
- Used a formula to produce a graph

If you did this task in two hours or less and have met each of the requirements listed above you should be ready to take the CLAIT graphics/plotting assessment.

TASK 5

WHAT'S THIS TASK FOR?

This task, while covering all the CLAIT graphics/ plotting objectives, is presented in a different format, i.e. plans and graphs are provided as the source of information.

PART 1

046, 048, 050

1 Load your drawing program.
2 In this part of the assignment you are asked to design the layout of a kitchen.

057
060

Refer to the plan which shows the outline of a kitchen. Draw the outline as shown including the labels. Design the units, store them and then position them as shown.

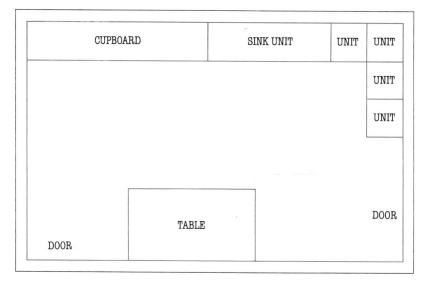

049

047

3 Shade the cupboard and the sink unit.

4 Print your plan.

062, 063

5 A new table has been bought to replace the square one. It is circular, and is to be placed in the centre of the kitchen. Change the plan to show this.

6 Print your finished plan.

062, 063

PART 2

051, 054

1 Load your pie-chart program which is to be used to display the costs of services/utilities.

057

2 Generate a pie chart as shown below, but shade the segments and add labels and numeric values to each.

060

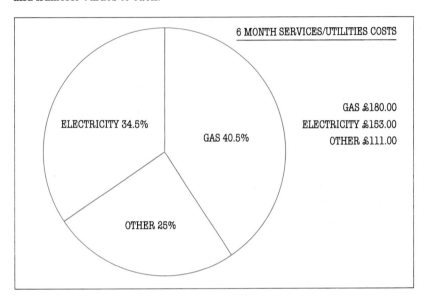

6 MONTH SERVICES/UTILITIES COSTS

GAS 40.5%

ELECTRICITY 34.5%

OTHER 25%

GAS £180.00
ELECTRICITY £153.00
OTHER £111.00

3 Load the printer with paper and set to top of form, check the printer is on-line and print your pie chart.

061, 062, 063

4 Load your histogram/bar chart program which you will use to display the monthly costs of services/utilities.

057

052, 054

5 Generate a histogram/bar chart as shown below; but select your own shading/pattern/colour

060

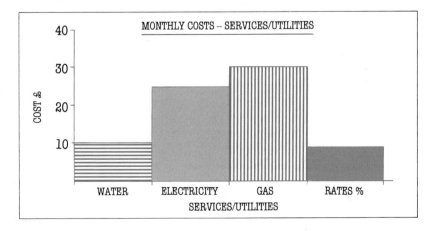

MONTHLY COSTS – SERVICES/UTILITIES

COST £

WATER   ELECTRICITY   GAS   RATES %

SERVICES/UTILITIES

6 Print your histogram/bar chart.

062, 063

7 Load the graph program which you will use to display the average number of units to be installed depending on the space available.

053, 054

8 Generate a line graph as shown below: each unit is 500 square millimetres.

057

060

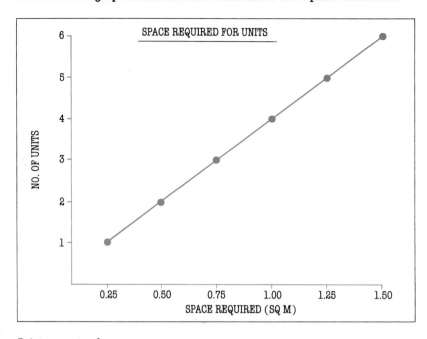

9 Print your graph.

062, 063

10 Load your graph program which can use a formula.

057

054, ★055

11 Generate a graph using a formula to show the cost of fitting a new kitchen (as shown below).
The cost of each unit plus fitting is £150.
The formula to be used is $Y = X \star 150$

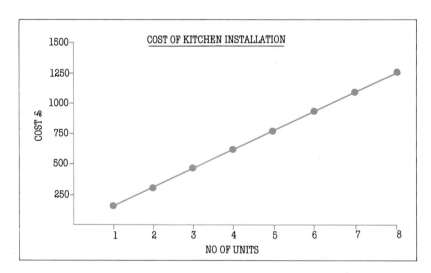

12 Print your graph.

062, 063

SELF-ASSESSMENT: TASK 5

DID I DO IT CORRECTLY?

- Drew the outline plan of the kitchen
- Changed the shape of the table
- Stored the shapes of the units
- Coloured or shaded the cupboard and sink unit
- Used text to label the drawing as shown
- Used a variety of prepared data to produce:
  - a pie chart
  - a histogram
  - a graph
- Used text to label the graphs/charts
- Used a formula to produce a graph

If you did this task in two hours or less and have met each of the requirements listed above you should be ready to take the CLAIT graphics/plotting assessment.

7 THE COMPUTER SYSTEM
OVERVIEW

WHAT IS A COMPUTER SYSTEM?

A computer system is a combination of related electronic machines. It is made up of a **processor** to perform the arithmetical and logical operations, and **peripherals**, which usually include an input device, a screen, disc drives or storage facilities and a printer.

NETWORK TERMINALS

SHARED DISC STORAGE SYSTEM

COMPUTER TERMS

NETWORKS

A network is a set of computers or terminals (workstations) that are linked together by communication lines. These communication lines can be special cables or the wires in the public telephone system. The workstations on a network usually share peripherals such as printers and the central data store.

INPUTTING

This is the entering of 'raw' data or information into a processing system. Several devices can be used to input data to computer systems, e.g. keyboards, mice, light pens, joysticks. **Input** is also used to mean any information that is entered into the computer.

PROCESSING

Processing is:

- conversion of data into a form recognisable by the computer;
- calculation by the computer;
- reconversion for output.

CENTRALISED PRINTER

WHY USE A COMPUTER SYSTEM?

Computer systems are excellent at calculating at very high speeds and storing and retrieving data. Computers are capable of carrying out a sequence of instructions automatically and, since computers are reprogrammable, the sets of instructions, or programs, can be changed so that the computer system can perform many different sets of tasks. Computers are used mainly for calculating, data handling, information processing, art and graphic design, controlling devices, monitoring test results and as a means of instruction.

STAND-ALONE MICRO-COMPUTER

MODEM

STORAGE

When information has been entered into the processor, it can be stored in the data store. Saved information can be retrieved for updating or reference.

OUTPUTTING

When data or information has been processed, the results can be **output** in several ways, e.g. displayed on the screen, printed, produced in graphical form, plotted or magnetically coded. **Output** is also used to mean any information produced by the computer.

COMMUNICATION

Computer communication refers to the passing of information between peripherals along communication lines. These may either be part of a computer system or be the public telephone system. A modem may be needed to send the information along the communication line.

USING COMPUTERS

On pages 84 – 8 you will find a list of the RSA CLAIT objectives relating to the general skills of operating computers. Under the remarks column is a brief explanation of each of these. You should read the remarks and then find out and note down in the final column how to carry out each operation on your system.

STARTING UP AND CLOSING DOWN

Profile Sentence P28	Start up a computer system; load the program and data; close down the system.

OBJECTIVE	REMARKS	HOW DO I DO IT?
056 Power up in correct sequence	It is necessary to power up (set the computer going) in the correct sequence. The computer works by following a set of instructions, and if this is not entered exactly, the system will not operate. Each system will be powered up in a different manner. Some are programmed to load a program when they are powered up.	
057 Load a program	When your system has been powered up, you will need to load the program you wish to use. This process depends on the system you are using.	
058 Load data into the system	When you have loaded your program, worked on a file and saved it, you may wish to load that data back into the system for further work.	
059 Close down the system in correct sequence	Before you close down your system, you must take out any discs that are in the disc drives so that you do not lose the data on them. It is also vital to exit from (leave) the program in the correct manner so that files are not left open, and to ensure the data has been saved. You should switch off all the component parts of your system in the order described by your tutor/ manual, and finally switch off the power at the mains supply.	

USING AN INPUT DEVICE

Profile Sentence P29   Use an input device.

OBJECTIVE

060   Use the keyboard or other input device to enter data

REMARKS

In order to process information using a computer system, you must first enter the information or data into the computer.

The most common means of input is with the keyboard. Most computer keyboards are standard 'QWERTY' keyboards i.e. with the same layout as most typewriters. Most computers have additional keys such as Shift Lock, Caps Lock, Control and the Alt key, and also other special **function keys** whose 'function' depends on the program which is in use.

You can sometimes identify the function of any of the keys by looking at the corresponding label on the screen once the program is loaded.

Some computer keyboards also have a separate numeric keypad.

Although the keyboard is the most common input device, there are other devices such as touch pads (often used with graphics applications) and touch-sensitive screens (the function or command is carried out when the operator merely touches a label or specific point on the VDU).

One of the newest devices for program interaction is the mouse. This allows the user to move the cursor around the screen more rapidly than by pressing the cursor keys. A function or command is activated by moving the cursor to point to a position on the screen, and then pressing a key on the mouse.

HOW DO I DO IT?

USING THE PRINTER

Profile Sentence P30   Use a printer.

When you have entered your data into the computer, processed it and saved it, you will want to see the results of your work. This can be seen in two ways: either you can output to the VDU and view your work 'on screen', or you can output your work to a printer and obtain 'hard copy'.

OBJECTIVE	REMARKS	HOW DO I DO IT?
061 Load paper into printer, set paper and printer to the top of a form.	The loading of paper into the printer can be automatic or manual. Most printers give an audible signal when they run out of paper. Most printers have to be taken off-line so that the paper can be positioned at the top of a form (i.e. at the top of a page). This makes sure that the printing, particularly on continuous stationery, does not go over the edge of the page or run across the perforations. There will normally be two other buttons to help you to position the paper - they are labelled **LF** (line feed) and **FF** (form feed).	
062 Check printer is on-line	'On-line' means 'ready for use'. Information that is sent from the computer will not be printed until the printer is on-line.	
063 Output hard copy	You should be able to produce a hard copy of the work you have carried out on the computer, so that it can be sent to other people or stored as a paper version.	

You may have heard some other terms used in connection with printers, for example impact (which touch the paper) and non-impact (which do not touch the page), tractor feed and friction feed.

You may wish to do some research into the types of printer available. You might include laser printers, line printers, dot-matrix printers and ink-jet printers. It might be interesting to do a comparative study covering:

- speed,
- quality of output,
- cost.

STORAGE SYSTEMS

Profile Sentence P31 Use a disc storage system.
OR
Profile Sentence P32 Use a tape storage system.

If you are using a disc storage system, the procedure you have to follow will depend on the type of system it is; i.e. whether it has a hard disc, dual or single disc drive, and on the type of operating system. You will need to check with your tutor or the manual whether you are using 'directories' or 'user areas'.

OBJECTIVE

REMARKS

HOW DO I DO IT?

064 Format a blank disc or select an empty user area

Before you can use a disc it must be formatted to suit your system. The manufacturer of the disc does not prepare it for use on any particular computer system or for a specific operating system.
   Formatting prepares the disc for use so that the information can be stored on it in a logical manner and accessed quickly and easily.
   Once a disc is formatted for use on a system it will not require formatting again (unless you wish to use it on a different system).

065 Copy a file from one disc to another, or copy a file from one user area to another

It may be necessary to copy a file from one disc/user area to another disc/user area so that you can keep a copy of a file. You may require a second copy of your file for security purposes, or to carry out further work on the file without altering the original file. The exact process of copying will depend on your operating system.

066 List the directory of files available

If you wish to see a list of the files on your disc, you will have to get a catalogue or directory of the disc. The correct command will depend on the operating system you are using.

067 Erase a file from disc or user area

It is also useful to list your files to check that a file has been copied or deleted. You may wish to delete files from your disc, for example if you have finished with the data, or if you require additional space to store new data.

068 Load a file from tape

If you are using a tape storage system it is necessary to position the tape at the place where the file has been saved before you load the file. If you do not specify a file name it will load the next file on the tape.

069 Save a program on tape

If you wish to save a file on tape you will have to specify the file name and position the tape at the correct place.

BACKING UP DATA

> **Profile Sentence P 33**   Operate a simple system to ensure the backing of data.

OBJECTIVE

070   Operate a simple system to ensure the backing of data

REMARKS

It is vital that you keep at least one back-up copy of your work on a separate disc, and advisable to store these security backup discs in a different place to your originals. If a disc in use is then corrupted or lost you will at least be able to recover some of the lost data.

Discs should be stored in the correct environment, with regard to temperature, security, etc. Storage boxes which will protect your disc from damage are available, and it is wise to follow the advice concerning handling that is printed on the disc labels or the paper envelopes in which the discs are held. Always lock discs in a secure place to protect them from corruption—both accidental and deliberate.

HOW DO I DO IT?

_____

_____

_____

_____

_____

_____

_____

_____

_____

_____

THE COMPUTER AS A COMMUNICATING DEVICE

> **Profile Sentence P34**   Use a computer as a communicating device.

OBJECTIVE

071   Connect the computer using appropriate hardware and software to
(a)   send information to, OR
(b)   receive or retrieve information from,
another source (e.g. another computer) locally through a network or remotely through an external communications system.

REMARKS

For this objective you have to use the computer either to send a message to, or to receive a message from, another source. This can be achieved in a number of ways, some of which are listed below:

- electronic mail
- Prestel
- Times Educational Network
- through a modem to another room/site
- on a network by sending a message from one station to a pre-determined user

HOW DO I DO IT?

_____

_____

_____

_____

_____

_____

_____

_____

This scheme provides both Stage I certification for those who fulfil the criteria specified on page 92 and profile certification for those who are unable, or do not wish, to fulfil full Stage I requirements.

Target population: anyone who wishes to be able to use computers and information technology. This scheme also provides a comprehensive basis for those intending to go on to specialised or more advanced studies.

Aim: to assess the candidate's ability to use computers and information technology effectively in common applications.

Topics	Assessment Objectives	Profile Sentences
	Candidates must be able to demonstrate ability to	

1 Applications of computers and information technology

NB: For a profile certificate, candidates must attempt at least one of the following Applications; for award of a Stage I certificate candidates must meet all the Objectives on at least three of the Applications as well as all the Objectives in Section 2.

Topics		Assessment Objectives		Profile Sentences
(a) A Word Processing package	01	**ENTER** text		
	02	**LOAD** text	P1	Enter, load and save text
	03	**SAVE** text		
	04	**INSERT** words		
	05	**INSERT** paragraph		
	06	**DELETE** words	P2	Insert/delete/replace words; insert/delete paragraphs
	07	**DELETE** paragraph		
	08	**REPLACE** words		
	09	**CHANGE** margins	P3	Change margins
		FORMAT printout:		
	⋆010	line-spacing	⋆P4	Change layout
	⋆011	justification (on/off)		
(b) A Spreadsheet package	012	**ENTER** text		
	013	**ENTER** numeric data	P5	Enter and edit text and numeric data
	014	**DELETE** entries		
	015	**REPLACE** entries		
	016	**REPLICATE** entries	P6	Replicate in a spreadsheet
	017	**CHANGE** the format	P7	Change the format
	018	**USE** a formula	P8	Use formulae
	⋆019	**ADD** a row or column	⋆P9	Extend the spreadsheet
	⋆020	**PROJECT** new values		

Topics		Assessment Objectives		Profile Sentences
(c) A Database package	021	**SET UP** files containing alphabetic and numeric fields within the record	P10	Set up a database
	022	**ENTER** data		
	023	**ADD** records	P11	Enter data and edit the database
	024	**DELETE** records		
	025	**EDIT** records		
	026	**SORT** records by a keyfield	P12	Formulate selection procedures for target records
	027	**SEARCH** records by a keyfield		
	★028	**PRINT** selected fields	★P13	Print selected fields
	★029	**SEARCH** on more than one criterion	★P14	Search on more than one criterion
(d) A Videotex System	030	**LOG ON** to a viewdata and/or teletext system	P15	Log on to a videotex system
	031	**TRACE** pages on a specific topic	P16	Trace pages on a specific topic
	032	**AMEND** a directory of pages available	P17	Amend a directory of pages available
	033	**EDIT** a page	P18	Edit a page
	034	**CHANGE THE ROUTEING** of a page	P19	Change the routeing of a page
		COMPOSE a new page using techniques of:		
	★035	coloured text	★P20	Compose a new page using a variety of techniques
	★036	double height characters		
	★037	flashing		
	★038	graphics		
	★039	background filling		
(e) A Business/Accounting package	040	**ENTER** a variety of business information relevant to the package	P21	Enter information
(Packages most suitable for this are: General ledger; Purchase ledger; Sales ledger; Payroll; Stock control)	041	**SEARCH** the package for information	P22	Search the package for information
	042	**ADD** records	P23	Change file details
	043	**DELETE** records		
	044	**CHANGE** records		
	★045	**PRODUCE** a report on specified information	★P24	Produce a report on specified information
(f) A Graphics/Plotting package (It *may* be necessary to use more than one package for this section.)				
(i) a drawing system	046	**DRAW** shapes/symbols	P25	Draw, change, label and store shapes/symbols
	047	**CHANGE** shapes/symbols		
	048	**STORE** shapes/symbols		
	049	**COLOUR OR SHADE** sections		
	050	**USE** text to label drawings		
(ii) graphical representation		**USE** a variety of prepared data to produce:		
	051	pie charts	P26	Produce graphical outputs from numeric data
	052	histograms		
	053	graphs		
	054	**USE** text to label graphs/charts		
	★055	**USE** a formula to produce a graph	★P27	Use a formula to produce a graph

Topics	Assessment Objectives		Profile Sentences	

2 Computers and information technology

(a) Using the computer system

056 **POWER UP** in correct sequence
057 **LOAD** a program
058 **LOAD** data into the system
059 **CLOSE DOWN** the system in correct sequence

P28 Start up a computer system; load the program and data; close down the system.

(b) Using components of the computer system

(i) Input device

060 **USE** the keyboard or other input device to enter data

P29 Use an input device

(ii) Output device

USE the printer to output information:
061 **LOAD** paper into printer, set paper and printer to the top of a form
062 **CHECK** printer is on-line
063 **OUTPUT** hard copy

P30 Use a printer

(iii) Storage media

Either

064 **FORMAT** a blank disc or select an empty user area
065 **COPY** a file from one disc to another or copy a file from one user area to another
066 **LIST** the directory of files available
067 **ERASE** a file from disc or user area

P31 Use a disc storage system

or

or

068 **LOAD** a file from tape
069 **SAVE** a program on tape

P32 Use a tape storage system

070 **OPERATE** a simple system to ensure the backing of data

P33 Operate a simple system to ensure the backing of data

(c) Using a computer as a communicating device

071 **CONNECT** the computer, using appropriate hardware and software to
(a) send information to, **OR**
(b) receive or retrieve information from,
another source (e.g. another computer) locally through a network or remotely through an external communications system.

P34 Use a computer as a communicating device

SCHEME OF ASSESSMENT

Assignments set in the *contexts* of the six Applications (I (a) – (f)) will also test all the Objectives of Section 2 in integrative tasks. Centres have the option of using Assignments set by the RSA or of devising their own Assignments. Assessment will be carried out locally, by marking against an RSA checklist, and a sample of the assessed work from each centre will be checked by the RSA.

CRITERIA OF ASSESSMENT

To qualify for any Profile Sentence candidates must satisfy the Assessor in all the Assessment Objectives specified for it in the syllabus above.

Objectives relating to the entry of data must be carried out to a level of accuracy equivalent to no more than 3 errors per Assignment.

Objectives relating to the manipulation and alteration of data must be carried out with complete accuracy.

Objectives in Section 2 (e.g. relating to the use of software instructions to carry out tasks such as copying, printing, loading data) are either carried out correctly (in which case the candidate has met the criteria) or not carried out correctly (in which case the criteria have not been met).

CERTIFICATION

Certificates will be awarded as follows:

(a) Candidates who qualify for one or more of the Profile Sentences will be awarded a profile listing of all the sentences in which they have demonstrated competence.

(b) Candidates who qualify for all the Profile Sentences, except those marked with an asterisk, in at least *three* of the Applications of Section 1 and all the Objectives in Section 2 will be awarded a Certificate denoting a Pass at Stage I.

(c) Those who further qualify for all the asterisked Profile Sentences in three Applications of Section 1 will be awarded an endorsement for a Distinction at Stage I.